BAKING BETTER BREADS

There is no substitute for home-baked bread, and here is a
fascinating range of recipes — all with the emphasis on
wholegrains — which shows the wealth of variety that exists
within the general theme of bread baking.

Hot Cross buns   425°F

½ oz yeast   2oz sugar
1 tsp sugar   2 tsp spice
½ pt. warm milk   2 oz sultanas
1 lb plain flour
1 tsp salt.   Glaze :   2 Tbs sugar
¾ oz veg.fat   2 Tbs water

Cream yeast & sugar until liquid & add the
milk. Sprinkle a little flour on top, cover
& put in warm place for ~15mins.
Sift rest of flour into bowl, with salt. Rub
in fat. Add sugar, fruit & spices & then the
yeast mixture. If necessary add more milk
to make a soft dough. Knead well. Cover &
leave to rise til double in bulk. Knead lightly,
shape into buns & place on greased trays.
Cut a cross on top & leave to rise again until
double the size.
Bake until they sound hollow when tapped
(about 10 mins) While still hot brush with
glaze made by bringing sugar & water to the
boil. Use hot.

BAKING
BETTER BREADS

by

RACHAEL HOLME

Illustrated by Clive Birch

THORSONS PUBLISHERS LIMITED
Wellingborough, Northamptonshire

First published 1983

British Library Cataloguing in Publication Data

Holme, Rachael
  Baking better breads.
  1. Bread
  I. Title
  641.8'15   TX769

ISBN 0-7225-0762-3

Printed in Great Britain by
Richard Clay (The Chaucer Press) Ltd,
Bungay, Suffolk

CONTENTS

INTRODUCTION

The best reason for baking your own bread is undoubtedly that it tastes better than the shop-bought variety. However fresh you buy your bread from the baker, it cannot compete with the advantages of making your own. This is because all commercial bakers use standard mixtures of ingredients to produce exactly the same type of loaf day after day after day; whereas, in your own kitchen you can add whatever takes your fancy to your dough. If you happen to have a few raisins left in the bottom of the bag, you can throw them into your bread mix for a bit of extra flavour. Any left-over pieces such as cheese, cream, a few nuts or even orange rind can be incorporated into the dough, thus making use of any excess food that you may not otherwise be able to use. At the same time you are creating your own delicious and interesting recipes and producing the best possible quality bread for you and your family to eat.

The delicious fragrance of bubbling yeast in the kitchen is only the start of the adventure. The aroma of freshly baked bread as you take it from the oven is well worth the effort of kneading and raising the dough. The first taste of your own crusty baked loaves will lure you into trying some more adventurous recipes, and the simple instructions in this book will help you to bake beautiful bread professionally and painlessly.

Flour
The most commonly used grain for baking bread is wheat. There are a variety of types of wheat available, but bakers generally prefer a 'hard' wheat grain with a high gluten content for breadmaking as

this type absorbs more water and gives a greater volume, making a lighter loaf. Wheat flour commonly comes in three grades:

*1) *Wholewheat:*   which contains 100% of the grain with nothing added and nothing taken away.

*2) *Wheatmeal:*   which contains 81% or 85% of the grain, with some of the bran and wheatgerm removed. (Half way between wholewheat and white).

 3) *White:*   this consists of only the starchy part of the wheat grain and has all of the germ and bran fibre removed.

Apart from wheat there are many other types of grains which can be milled and added to wheat flour to add flavour and make your bread more interesting and appealing. Rye flour is another of the most commonly used. This has a distinct flavour and dark colour and makes a good loaf when used half and half with wheat flour. Barley flour is a sweet, moist flour and blends happily with wheat flour to give bread a more cake-like consistency and a sweeter flavour. The addition of maize flour (cornmeal) makes bread more crumbly and crunchy. Bread made with brown rice flour tends to be very dense, but it is exceedingly good sliced very, very thinly and toasted. When millet flour is incorporated into bread it gives it a much fuller flavour and tastes richer.

There are a variety of other dry ingredients which can be added in varying quantities to affect the flavour of the bread. Extra wheatgerm, bran, whole soaked rye or wheat grains, cracked wheat or any type of flaked grain all give their own distinctive flavours and textures to bread. Granary flour is a particular mixture of 81% wheat flour, malted wheat flakes and sometimes malted rye flakes, rye flour and a few whole rye grains. This has a chewy, slightly sweet flavour and is gaining in popularity throughout the country because, while having the appearance of 'brown bread' it is noticeably light and spongy in consistency. Experimentation is a virtue in cookery, and as far as bread is concerned, anything goes.

*Both of these also go under the name of 'wholemeal' to indicate any type of 'brown' flour.

Yeast

Yeast is a microscopic fungus, a living plant which needs food, liquid and warmth to activate it. As the yeast bubbles away, it gives off carbon dioxide which makes the dough rise. There are two sorts of yeast which are readily available for bread making. The first, and best in my opinion, is fresh cake yeast. This feels rather like putty but it has a pleasant, musty aroma. This type of yeast stores well in a refrigerator for a couple of weeks, but it will also freeze for up to a year. If you can't find a source of fresh yeast, then the dried variety will suffice. This is packaged as tiny granules in tins, or in specially prepared paper sachets, and will keep for up to six months unopened.

All yeast mixtures need warmth if they are to grow and bubble as required. Yeast works best at between 98° and 110°F (36.5 and 43°C). Temperatures over this will kill it so be careful not to overheat it. The yeast mixture should be left in a warm place to work, protected from draughts — it is a good idea to cover it with a clean cloth for this reason. Anyone possessing a Rayburn or Aga cooker has the ideal place to let yeast work. The top shelf above the hotplates on these types of cookers is the ideal situation.

Although yeast is used in most bread recipes, it is not necessarily a vital ingredient, and some recipes for unyeasted bread are included in this book.

Liquids

A variety of liquids can be used to mix a bread dough, but the most common is water. The most important point to remember here is temperature. The water must be warm enough to encourage the yeast to work, but it mustn't be too hot or it will kill it. When the yeasty liquid is sufficiently bubbly the rest of the liquid can be added to it, and the whole amount can then be added to the flour in one go. (Remember that extra flour can easily be incorporated into a slack dough, whereas it is almost impossible to knead in extra liquid to a dough that is too stiff.)

Other liquid ingredients can be substituted for the water in a bread recipe. Milk is a commonly used alternative, which makes the bread more nutritious. Beaten eggs can be used as part of the liquid, giving added richness to the finished product. Fruit juices can be used to impart a more interesting flavour, and yogurt can be added to make a surprisingly light, springy bread. Other liquid flavourings such as lemon juice, honey or vinegar are also added at this stage.

Fats
Any type of fat or oil added to a bread dough has the effect of enriching it and so helps to keep it moist. Hard fats such as butter can be added in two ways: they can be melted and added at the same time as the liquid, or they can be rubbed into the dry ingredients before the liquid is mixed in. Polyunsaturated margarines and vegetable oils are just as effective, as well as being better for you.

Sweetness
Some form of sugar has to be added to the yeast and warm water. This acts as food for the yeast, to make it grow. Raw cane sugar and honey are the most commonly used ingredients for this, but malt extract, molasses or maple syrup can also be used for different flavours.

Extra Ingredients
There are many different special extras that can be added to a bread dough to make it more interesting and different. All sorts of herbs and spices can be used, each one imparting its own unique flavour. Caraway seeds or dill seeds are traditionally used with rye bread. Poppy seeds make a good decoration sprinkled on top and also lend a nutty flavour to the bread. Sesame seeds are my favourite, especially in a milk loaf. All manner of dried fruits and nuts can be incorporated. Also cheese, and some vegetables such as onions, potatoes or pumpkin are interesting to experiment with. Finely grated lemon rind or orange rind is another of my favourites. Sea salt is used in most bread recipes, although it shouldn't be used in too large a quantity as it inhibits the growth of the yeast.

Mixing

The majority of recipes in this book start by dissolving the yeast in a liquid, then adding any other ingredients, and last of all by mixing in the flour. Any large mixing bowl will do to mix the dough, although I prefer a pottery one as once it is warmed through it will stay warm, and it is ideal to leave the dough in for the first rising. Making bread is an activity which needs lots of warmth, so it is helpful to warm all the utensils before you start. My husband's bread making motto goes as follows: 'Warm the bowl, warm your hands, then warm your heart'.

Kneading

It is necessary to knead the dough so that it strengthens and develops the gluten, turning it into a product capable of gaining a reasonable rise. You need lots of extra flour to knead properly, so start by covering your board or kneading surface with two or three ounces of extra wholemeal flour. Turn the dough out onto this, and sprinkle a bit more flour over the top. Start kneading by folding the dough towards you, pushing down and away from you with the palm of your hand. Rotate the dough a quarter turn and continue kneading. Repeat this action for at least ten minutes or longer, until you feel the dough is really smooth and elastic and no longer sticky.

Lots of electric mixers have dough hooks, which can do all this work for you, with no effort on your part, in about three or four minutes. Make sure the machine runs on a low speed, and take good note of recommended maximum quantities — if you put too much dough in at a time you run the risk of damaging your machine. The dough now needs to be left to rise before it can briefly be kneaded again or 'knocked back' and shaped for the tins.

Rising

The length of time it takes for the dough to rise depends mainly on the temperature in which it is left. If it is left in a fairly warm place it will probably only need about an hour to double in size, whereas if left in the fridge it will take a whole day. I find the most convenient place to leave my bread to rise is on top of a tumble-drier in action.

While the clothes inside are being tumbled about to dry, the top of the drier reaches just the right degree of warmth to raise the dough to perfection. Other more commonly used places include the airing cupboard, on top of a radiator shelf or inside a switched off oven.

To prepare the dough for rising, shape it into a ball and roll it in flour. Put it into a large bowl or other large container, which should be large enough to allow the dough to double in bulk at least. Cover this with a clean tea-towel or plastic film and set it in the warmth to rise. Check the dough after about three-quarters of an hour. When it has more or less doubled in size, you can take it out of the bowl for the final kneading or 'knocking back'. Just knead it gently for a few more minutes until it regains its smooth, elastic consistency. Then shape the loaves and place them in their tins. The second rising takes much less time than the first, usually about half an hour or even less. Treat the dough in the tins in the same way as for the first rising. Keep your eyes on the dough so as not to overprove the loaves. When they have doubled in size again or reached the tops of their tins, they are ready to bake.

Baking

Most breads start off being baked at a fairly high temperature, around 400°F/200°C (Gas Mark 6), for a short time. Generally, the temperature is lowered after five to ten minutes to around 350°/180°C (Gas Mark 4) for the remainder of the cooking time. Sometimes it is a good idea to put a bowl of hot water at the bottom of the oven. This turns into steam in the heat of the oven and is said to improve the quality of the bread, giving it a more professional appearance and texture.

You can tell if a loaf is thoroughly cooked by tapping it gently on the bottom with your knuckles. If it is done, it will sound hollow.

Storing

Bread is undoubtedly best eaten on the day it is made, but for those of us who cannot be bothered to bake every day (me for one), some method of storage is essential. Most people possess the traditional metal or earthenware bread bin to keep bread in. This keeps out the flies and helps to retain some moisture, but it won't preserve the bread for any real length of time. If you want to make fresh bread last for several days, wrap it in clingfilm and store it in a cool place. This helps to retain more moisture. Certain breads keep better than others, so if you continually want your bread to last over several days, it's a good idea to stick to malt loaves, dark rye breads or loaves enriched with eggs, which generally are moister to start with and so keep longer anyway.

Freezing

If you need to keep bread for longer than a few days, or if you get into the habit of baking large quantities of bread at one session, you may wish to freeze some of it so that it is still fresh by the time you come to the end of the batch. This can be frozen ready-baked or as an unrisen dough. Whichever method you prefer, wrap the cooled bread or unrisen dough in silver foil or a plastic freezer bag and place it in the freezer. The ready-baked bread may be left for up to eight months, but don't keep unrisen dough in the freezer for more than three months. Expect unrisen dough to lose some of its rising potency after freezing; compensate for this by using 50% extra yeast when mixing the dough.

Loaves can also be frozen when only partly baked. This gives you the advantage of being able to produce hot, crusty bread with all the delicious aromas and smells that are traditionally associated with home baking, despite the fact that the loaf has been frozen previously. Bake the loaf in the same way as usual for the first 30 minutes. Take it out of the oven and let it cool completely in the tin. Freeze it still in the tin, then gently ease it out of the tin and wrap it as above. When you want to use it, slip it back into the original tin while still frozen and let it thaw. Bake for another 20 to 30 minutes at 350°F/180°C (Gas Mark 4).

It is sometimes useful to freeze your loaves ready-sliced. Then you can just take out one or two slices when you need them and keep the remainder frozen until required. Slice the loaf thinly and open-freeze the slices on a flat tray. Place them in a polythene bag, seal and return to the freezer. These slices can be thawed in the usual way, or can be popped straight into a toaster for instant defrosting.

Any stale or left-over bread can be made into breadcrumbs and frozen. Breadcrumbs have the advantage of staying separate when frozen so you can use just as much as you need at a time. They can be used for making home-made stuffings, bread sauce, puddings or for using with beaten eggs to coat certain foods before frying. Alternatively, mixed with a little raw cane sugar and dotted with butter they make an excellent topping for fruit crumbles.

If you prefer, you can cut stale or excess fresh bread into cubes and fry them lightly in a little vegetable oil to make *croûtons* for soup. Pack them in plastic bags and seal. Thaw them in a hot oven, uncovered on a flat baking tray for five minutes.

Leave plenty of time to thaw whole loaves before use; from three to six hours is best, depending on the size of the loaf. It is a good idea to get into the habit of removing bread from the freezer at night, as then it will be thawed ready for breakfast the next day. If you need to thaw it more quickly than this, put it into a very low oven, along with a bowl of boiling water (so that the crust will stay moist).

BASIC BREAD RECIPES

BASIC WHOLEMEAL BREAD
(Makes 2 large loaves)

Imperial (Metric)	American
1 dessertspoonful honey	1 tablespoonful honey
1½ oz (40g) fresh yeast	3½ tablespoonsful fresh yeast
1¼ pints (650ml) warm water	3¼ cupsful warm water
2½ lb (1¼ kilos) wholemeal flour	10 cupsful wholemeal flour
1 dessertspoonful sea salt	1 tablespoonful sea salt
2 tablespoonsful vegetable oil	2½ tablespoonsful vegetable oil

1. Cream the honey and yeast together with a fork until they are well blended and there are no lumps of yeast left.

2. Add ½ pint (¼ litre) of the warm water and mix well. Cover the container with a clean cloth and set it in a warm place for 10-15 minutes until it starts to froth and bubble.

3. Meanwhile, sieve the flour and salt into a large mixing bowl.

4. When the yeast mixture is ready, beat the oil into it with a fork and pour it onto the flour. Add the remaining warm water and mix everything together until the dough is formed.

5. Turn the dough out onto a well floured board and knead it for about 10 minutes until it starts to feel smoother and more elastic, adding a little extra flour if necessary.

6. Place the dough back into the mixing bowl and cover it with a clean cloth. Put it in a warm place for about an hour or so, or until it has doubled in bulk.

7. Turn the dough out onto a floured board and knead it again for another few minutes, then divide the dough into two equal pieces and shape them into smooth loaves. Put them into well oiled tins and set them in a warm place, covered with a cloth, to rise again.

8. When the dough reaches the tops of the tins, place them in a hot oven at 400°F/200°C (Gas Mark 6) for 10 minutes, then turn down the heat to 350°F/180°C (Gas Mark 4) and continue to bake for a further 30-40 minutes.

QUICK, UNKNEADED WHOLEMEAL BREAD
(Makes 1 large loaf)

Any bread recipe which leaves out the kneading process produces a loaf which is coarser in texture and more dense; but if you want to make your own bread and just can't face all that kneading, then this recipe is for you. It makes a quite acceptable loaf, although it should all be used up on the day it is made as it does not keep well for any length of time.

Imperial (Metric)	American
1 oz (25g) dried yeast	2½ tablespoonsful dried yeast
½ pint (¼ litre) warm water	1⅓ cupsful warm water
1 dessertspoonful honey	1 tablespoonful honey
1 lb 6 oz (650g) wholemeal flour	5½ cupsful wholemeal flour
1 dessertspoonful sea salt	1 tablespoonful sea salt

1. Dissolve the dried yeast in the warm water, stirring it until it is all absorbed. Then add the honey and mix well. Set aside in the warmth for 10-15 minutes.

2. Mix the flour and salt together, and set half of it aside in a separate bowl. Add the bubbly yeast mixture to one half of the flour and mix it in well to form a thick batter. Whisk this by hand for about 10 minutes, or use an electric whisk for a couple of minutes.

3. Add the rest of the flour and mix to form a smooth dough. Shape the dough into a smooth ball and put it into a well oiled bread tin and leave to rise in a warm place for ½-¾ hour, until it reaches the top of the tin.

4. Bake at 400°F/200°C (Gas Mark 6) for 10 minutes, then turn the heat down to 350°F/180°C (Gas Mark 4) and continue to bake for a further 30-40 minutes.

SOURDOUGH LOAF
(Makes 1 large loaf)

Sourdough Starter:

Imperial (Metric)	American
1 dessertspoonful honey	1 tablespoonful honey
1 oz (25g) fresh yeast	2½ tablespoonsful fresh yeast
½ pint (¼ litre) warm water	1⅓ cupsful warm water
6 oz (150g) wholemeal flour	1½ cupsful wholemeal flour

To add later:

Imperial (Metric)	American
10 oz (300g) wholemeal flour	2½ cupsful wholemeal flour
1½ dessertspoonsful sea salt	1 tablespoonful sea salt
1 dessertspoonful milk	1 tablespoonful milk

1. Cream the honey and the yeast together until no lumps are left, then add the warm water and stir well.

2. Mix in the first quantity of flour and whisk it in to form a batter. Leave this mixture in a large mixing bowl covered with a plate at room temperature from two to four days, depending on the strength of flavour required. You need to keep the batter in a large bowl to give it plenty of room to expand. Keep stirring it occasionally as the ingredients will separate and need to be reincorporated.

3. When you consider the batter to be ready, stir in the remaining wholemeal flour, salt and milk. Mix thoroughly to form a soft dough.

4. Turn the dough out onto a floured surface and knead for about 10 minutes until it appears putty-like. Place it in a large mixing bowl and cover with a cloth. Leave in a warm place to rise.

5. When it has just about doubled in bulk, turn the dough back out onto the floured surface and knead again for another few minutes. Have ready an oiled 2 lb loaf tin and press the dough into it. Leave to rise again somewhere warm until it fills the tin. Bake at 350°F/180°C (Gas Mark 4) for 45 minutes.

BREADS MADE WITH DIFFERENT GRAINS

SAVOURY BARLEY BREAD
(Makes 1 large loaf)

This recipe produces a fine-textured, flavoursome loaf which slices well and is good toasted.

Imperial (Metric)	American
1 dessertspoonful honey	1 tablespoonful honey
1½ oz (40g) fresh yeast	3½ tablespoonsful fresh yeast
½ pint (¼ litre) warm water	1⅓ cupsful warm water
10 oz (300g) wholemeal flour	2½ cupsful wholemeal flour
½ lb (¼ kilo) barley flour	1 cupful barley flour
1 teaspoonful sea salt	1 teaspoonful sea salt
1 tablespoonful real soya sauce	1 tablespoonful real soya sauce
A little beaten egg	A little beaten egg

1. Dissolve the honey and the fresh yeast in the warm water and set it aside in the warmth to start frothing.

2. Put the wholemeal flour, barley flour and salt in a large mixing bowl and mix them together. Make a well in the centre and pour the frothy yeast mixture into it with the soy sauce.

3. Mix well until the dough is formed. Knead vigorously for about 10 minutes or until you can feel the consistency of the dough changing to a more elastic state. Return the dough to the bowl, cover with a cloth and leave in a warm place to rise.

4. When fully risen, knead again for a further couple of minutes. Shape the loaf for the tin and place it into the tin which should be well oiled. Leave to rise again until the dough reaches the top of the tin.

5. Brush the top of the loaf with the beaten egg and bake at 400°F/200°C (Gas Mark 6) for 10 minutes. Reduce the heat to 350°F/180°C (Gas Mark 4) and bake for a further 20-30 minutes.

BARLEY AND HAZELNUT BREAD
(Makes 2 small loaves)

Imperial (Metric)	American
1 oz (25g) fresh yeast	2½ tablespoonsful fresh yeast
1 dessertspoonful molasses	1 tablespoonful molasses
Approx. ¾ pint (400ml) warm water	Approx. 2 cupsful warm water
1 lb 4 oz (600g) wholemeal flour	5 cupsful wholemeal flour
3 oz (75g) barley flour	½ cupful barley flour
1 dessertspoonful sea salt	1 tablespoonful sea salt
3 oz (75g) hazelnuts, chopped	⅔ cupful chopped hazelnuts

1. Cream the yeast and molasses together to form a smooth paste in a small bowl. Add the warm water and stir it in well. Leave the mixture covered in a warm place so that the yeast can start to work.

2. Place the wholemeal flour, barley flour, salt and chopped hazelnuts in a large mixing bowl. Mix them together and make a well in the centre.

3. Pour the frothy yeast mixture into the well and start mixing. When the dough has formed, turn it out onto a well floured board. Knead for about 10 minutes, using extra flour if it becomes too sticky.

4. Return the dough to the mixing bowl, cover it with a cloth and leave in the warmth for about ¾ hour or until it has doubled in size. Knead again for another couple of minutes, then divide the dough into two equal pieces. Shape each piece into a smooth-surfaced loaf shape and place them in two well oiled, small loaf tins.

5. Dissolve an extra teaspoonful of molasses in a little water and brush the tops of the loaves with it. Leave them to rise again in a warm place until the dough reaches the tops of the tins.

6.   Bake at 400°F/200°C (Gas Mark 6) for 10 minutes. Reduce the heat to 350°F/180°C (Gas Mark 4) and continue to bake for another 35 to 40 minutes.

7.   Leave the loaves to cool on a wire rack.

YOGURT RYE LOAF
(Makes 1 large loaf)

Imperial (Metric)	American
2 oz (50g) fresh yeast	¼ cupful fresh yeast
1 dessertspoonful honey	1 tablespoonful honey
¼ pint (150ml) warm water	⅔ cupful warm water
1 dessertspoonful sea salt	1 tablespoonful sea salt
14 oz (400g) wholemeal flour	3½ cupsful wholemeal flour
4 oz (100g) rye flour	1 cupful rye flour
¼ pint (150ml) natural yogurt	⅔ cupful natural yogurt
3 dessertspoonsful single cream	3 tablespoonsful single cream

1.   Cream the yeast and honey together until no lumps are left. Add the warm water and blend the mixture thoroughly, then leave it somewhere warm to allow the yeast to start working.

2.   Put all the dry ingredients together in a large mixing bowl and mix them together. Add the yeasty mixture, yogurt and cream and mix them in well. When the dough has formed, turn it out onto a floured board and knead it thoroughly for about 10 minutes. Put the dough back into the bowl, cover it with a cloth and leave it in a warm place until it has doubled in size.

3.   Knead the dough again for another few minutes, then shape it into a rough oblong. Place it in a well oiled 2 lb loaf tin and leave it somewhere warm again until the dough rises to the top of the tin.

4.   Bake at 350°F/180°C (Gas Mark 4) for 40 to 45 minutes.

SPICED BARLEY BREAD
(Makes 1 large loaf)

This makes a fairly heavy bread, but it has a really delicious flavour. Consequently, it is excellent sliced as thinly as possible and served with all manner of savoury spreads such as vegetable mayonnaise mixes etc.

Imperial (Metric)	American
1½ oz (40g) dried yeast	3½ tablespoonsful dried yeast
½ pint (¼ litre) warm water	1⅓ cupsful warm water
1 dessertspoonful honey	1 tablespoonful honey
1 teaspoonful ground nutmeg	1 teaspoonful ground nutmeg
2 teaspoonsful ground cinnamon	2 teaspoonsful ground cinnamon
1 tablespoonful ground mixed spice	1 tablespoonful ground mixed spice
1½ dessertspoonsful sea salt	1 tablespoonful sea salt
¾ lb (350g) wholemeal flour	3 cupsful wholemeal flour
6 oz (150g) barley flour	¾ cupful barley flour
4 dessertspoonsful milk	4 tablespoonsful milk

1. Dissolve the yeast in the warm water and then add the honey. Combine them well and leave the mixture in a warm place until it starts to froth.

2. Put all the remaining dry ingredients together in a large mixing bowl and mix them thoroughly. Make a well in the centre and pour in the yeasty liquid. Add the milk, and begin to mix everything together.

3. When the dough has formed, turn it out onto a floured board and knead it for 10 minutes or so. Return the dough to the bowl, cover it with a cloth and leave it in a warm spot for up to ¾ hour.

4. Knock back the dough for a further few minutes. Put it into a well oiled 2 lb bread tin and leave it in the warmth for up to an hour for the final rising.

5. When it reaches the top of the tin, bake at 350°F/180°C (Gas Mark 4) for 40 to 45 minutes.

RYE BREAD WITH DILL SEEDS
(Makes 1 large loaf)

Imperial (Metric)	American
1½ oz (40g) fresh yeast	3½ tablespoonsful fresh yeast
½ pint (¼ litre) warm water	1⅓ cupsful warm water
1 dessertspoonful honey	1 tablespoonful honey
½ lb (¼ kilo) rye flour	2 cupsful rye flour
10 oz (300g) wholemeal flour	2½ cupsful wholemeal flour
1 dessertspoonful sea salt	1 tablespoonful sea salt
½ oz (50g) dill seeds	1½ tablespoonsful dill seeds
A little milk	A little milk

1. Dissolve the yeast in the warm water and stir in the honey. Leave the mixture in a warm place for 10 to 15 minutes until it starts to froth.

2. Put the rye flour, wholemeal flour, salt and dill seeds into a large mixing bowl and stir them together. When the yeast mixture is ready, pour it into the centre of the flour and stir to form the dough. Roll the dough round with your hand until it is springy and kneadable, adding a little extra flour if the dough seems too sticky.

3. Turn the dough out onto a floured board and knead for 10 to 15 minutes, by which time it should feel smoother and more pliable. Put the dough back into the mixing bowl and cover it with a clean cloth then leave it in a warm place until it has doubled in size.

4. Knead again for another couple of minutes. Shape the dough carefully so that there are no cracks in the crust, and put it into a well oiled 2 lb loaf tin. Let it rise again to the top of the tin.

5. Brush the top of the crust with the extra milk and bake at 400°F/200°C (Gas Mark 6) for the first 10 minutes. Reduce the heat to 350°F/180°C (Gas Mark 4) and continue to bake the loaf for a further 30 to 40 minutes.

SAVOURY RYE AND MISO COB
(Makes 1 large cob loaf)

Imperial (Metric)	American
2 oz (50g) fresh yeast	¼ cupful fresh yeast
1 dessertspoonful malt extract	1 tablespoonful malt extract
½ pint (¼ litre) warm water	1⅓ cupsful warm water
4 oz (100g) rye flour	1 cupful rye flour
1 lb (½ kilo) wholemeal flour	4 cupsful wholemeal flour
1 dessertspoonful sea salt	1 tablespoonful sea salt
2 dessertspoonsful miso paste	2 tablespoonsful miso paste
A little beaten egg	A little beaten egg

1. Cream the yeast and malt extract together in a small bowl. Add the warm water, stir well and leave the mixture in a warm place to start frothing.

2. Put the rye flour, wholemeal flour and salt into a large mixing bowl and combine them well. When the yeast mixture looks good and frothy, stir the miso into it until it has all dissolved. Pour the liquid into the flour and mix well until the dough is formed.

3. Turn the dough out onto a well floured board and knead it for 10 to 15 minutes. Return the dough to the bowl, cover it with a cloth and leave it in a warm place until doubled in size.

4. Knock back the dough for another couple of minutes, then shape it into a smooth, round ball and place it on a flat baking tray. Cut a cross in the top using a sharp knife, then cover it with a cloth and leave it in a warm place until puffy and well risen.

5. Brush the crust all over with the beaten egg and bake at 400°F/200°C (Gas Mark 6) for 10 minutes. Then reduce the heat to 350°F/180°C (Gas Mark 4) and continue to bake for a further 20 minutes.

RICE BREAD
(Makes 1 large loaf)

Imperial (Metric)	American
1 dessertspoonful molasses	1 tablespoonful molasses
½ pint (¼ litre) warm water	1⅓ cupsful warm water
2 oz (50g) fresh yeast	¼ cupful fresh yeast
6 oz (150g) brown rice flour	1 cupful brown rice flour
14 oz (400g) wholemeal flour	3½ cupsful wholemeal flour
1 dessertspoonful sea salt	1 tablespoonful sea salt

1. Stir the molasses into the warm water until it dissolves. Then add the fresh yeast and blend it in with a fork. Leave this mixture in a warm place for 10 minutes or so until it starts to froth.

2. Put the brown rice flour, wholemeal flour and salt into a large mixing bowl and mix them together well. Add the frothy yeast mix and stir it in with a fork to form the dough. Turn this out onto a floured board and knead for 10 minutes until the dough becomes more elastic and pliable. Return the dough to the mixing bowl and set it aside in a warm place to double in size.

3. Knead the dough again for another couple of minutes and then shape it for the tin. Place it in a well oiled 2 lb loaf tin and leave it to rise somewhere warm. When it reaches the top of the tin, put it into a hot oven at 400°F/200°C (Gas Mark 6) for 10 minutes.

4. Turn the heat down to 350°F/180°C (Gas Mark 4) and continue to bake it for another 30 to 35 minutes.

WHOLEGRAIN BROWN RICE BREAD
(Makes 1 large loaf)

Imperial (Metric)	American
4 oz (100g) uncooked brown rice	½ cupful uncooked brown rice
2 oz (50g) fresh yeast	¼ cupful fresh yeast
1 dessertspoonful clear honey	1 tablespoonful clear honey
¼ pint (150ml) warm water	⅔ cupful warm water
1 lb 2 oz (550g) wholemeal flour	4½ cupsful wholemeal flour
1 dessertspoonful sea salt	1 tablespoonful sea salt
1 beaten egg	1 beaten egg
2 dessertspoonsful milk	2 tablespoonsful milk

1. Simmer the brown rice in plenty of boiling water until it is cooked but still slightly chewy. Drain and cool.

2. Cream the fresh yeast and honey together and add the warm water. Mix it in well and leave in a warm place to start bubbling.

3. Put the flour, salt and cooked brown rice into a large mixing bowl and stir them together. Add the beaten egg and milk to the frothy yeast mixture and whisk them together. Pour this liquid into the flour and mix it in well to form the dough.

4. Turn the dough out onto a well floured board and knead it for 10 to 15 minutes. Return the dough to the bowl, cover it with a cloth and leave it in a warm place to double in bulk.

5. Knock back the dough for another couple of minutes, then shape it for your tin.

6. Place the dough in a lightly oiled 2 lb loaf tin, cover it with a cloth and leave it in a warm place to rise again.

7. When the dough reaches the top of the tin, bake at 400°F/ 200°C (Gas Mark 6) for 10 minutes. Reduce the heat to 350°F/180°C (Gas Mark 4) and continue to bake for another 35 to 40 minutes until the loaf sounds hollow when tapped on the bottom.

BUCKWHEAT LOAF WITH HORSE-RADISH
(Makes 1 large loaf)

Imperial (Metric)	American
2 oz (50g) fresh yeast	¼ cupful fresh yeast
1 dessertspoonful clear honey	1 tablespoonful clear honey
½ pint (¼ litre) warm water	1⅓ cupsful warm water
14 oz (100g) wholemeal flour	3½ cupsful wholemeal flour
2 oz (50g) buckwheat flour	½ cupful buckwheat flour
1 teaspoonful sesame salt	1 teaspoonful sesame salt
2 teaspoonsful grated horse-radish root, very finely chopped	2 teaspoonsful grated horse-radish root, very finely chopped

1. Cream the fresh yeast and honey together in a small bowl. Stir in the warm water and leave the mixture in a warm place to start bubbling.

2. Place the flours, sesame salt and grated horse-radish root in a large mixing bowl and stir them thoroughly.

3. Pour the frothy yeast liquid into the flour and mix well to form a dough.

4. Turn the dough out onto a well floured board and knead well for about 10 minutes. Return the dough to the bowl, cover with a cloth and leave in a warm place until doubled in size.

5. Knock back the dough for another 2 or 3 minutes, then shape it for your tin. Place in a well oiled, large loaf tin, cover with a cloth and leave to rise again in a warm place.

6. When the dough reaches the top of the tin, bake at 400°F/200°C (Gas Mark 6) for 10 minutes. Then reduce the heat to 350°F/180°C (Gas Mark 4) and continue to bake for a further 35 to 40 minutes.

WHOLEGRAIN BUCKWHEAT BREAD
(Makes 1 large loaf)

Imperial (Metric)	American
½ oz (15g) dried yeast	1 tablespoonful dried yeast
1 dessertspoonful clear honey	1 tablespoonful clear honey
½ pint (¼ litre) warm water	1⅓ cupsful warm water
3 oz (75g) whole buckwheat grains	⅓ cupful whole buckwheat grains
1 lb (½ kilo) wholemeal flour	4 cupsful wholemeal flour
1 teaspoonful sea salt	1 teaspoonful sea salt

1. Mix together the dried yeast, honey and warm water in a small bowl and set it in the warmth to activate the yeast.

2. Simmer the whole buckwheat in plenty of boiling water in a saucepan over a gentle heat for about 10 minutes, until it is cooked but not mushy. Drain and leave it to cool.

3. Place the buckwheat, flour and salt in a large mixing bowl and stir them together. Add the frothy yeast liquid and mix it in well to form a dough.

4. Turn the dough out onto a well floured board and knead it for about 10 minutes until it feels more elastic and stretchy. Return the dough to the bowl, cover it with a cloth and leave it in a warm place until doubled in size.

5. Knock back the dough for another few minutes, then shape it for your tin. Place it in a lightly oiled, large loaf tin, cover with a cloth and leave it in the warmth until the crust reaches the top of the tin.

6. Bake at 400°F/200°C (Gas Mark 6) for 10 minutes. Reduce the heat to 350°F/180°C (Gas Mark 4) and continue to bake for a further 35 to 40 minutes.

YEASTED CORN BREAD
(Makes 1 large loaf)

Imperial (Metric)	American
1½ oz (40g) fresh yeast	3½ tablespoonsful fresh yeast
1 dessertspoonful honey	1 tablespoonful honey
½ pint (¼ litre) warm water	1⅓ cupsful warm water
1 beaten egg	1 beaten egg
½ lb (¼ kilo) fine maize flour	2 cupsful fine cornmeal
14 oz (400g) wholemeal flour	3½ cupsful wholemeal flour
2 teaspoonsful sea salt	2 teaspoonsful sea salt
2 oz (50g) skimmed milk powder	⅔ cupful skimmed milk powder

1. Put the yeast, honey, warm water and beaten egg into a small mixing bowl and beat them well with a fork or whisk until they are all well blended. Set this mixture aside in the warmth so that the yeast can start to work.

2. Meanwhile put the maize flour (cornmeal), wholemeal flour, salt and dried milk into a large mixing bowl and stir them together. When the yeast mixture is good and frothy, pour it into the flour mixture and blend it in with a fork.

3. Roll the mixture around with your hands until it forms a proper dough, then turn it onto a floured board and knead it for about 15 minutes. Put it back in the bowl, set it aside in a warm place and let it double in bulk.

4. Knock back the dough for a few minutes and then carefully shape it for the tin. Place it in a well greased 2 lb loaf tin and let it rise again until the top of the loaf just reaches the top of the tin. (It is important not to over-prove this type of bread, so don't let it rise any further.)

5. Bake at 400°F/200°C (Gas Mark 6) for half an hour, then turn down the heat to 350°F/180°C (Gas Mark 4) for a further 15 minutes. This bread is sweet, moist and yellowy and tends to be crumbly, so let it cool completely before slicing.

THREE GRAIN HERB LOAF
(Makes 1 large loaf)

Imperial (Metric)	American
1 dessertspoonful honey	1 tablespoonful honey
2 oz (50g) fresh yeast	¼ cupful fresh yeast
½ pint (¼ litre) warm water	1⅓ cupsful warm water
6 oz (150g) rye flour	1½ cupsful rye flour
2 oz (50g) buckwheat flour	½ cupful buckwheat flour
¾ lb (350g) wholemeal flour	3 cupsful wholemeal flour
1 dessertspoonful sea salt	1 tablespoonful sea salt
2 dessertspoonsful dried mixed herbs	2 tablespoonsful dried mixed herbs

1. Cream the honey and the yeast together until all the yeast has dissolved. Add the warm water and mix it in well. Set the mixture aside in a warm place, cover it with a clean cloth and leave for 10 to 15 minutes until the yeast starts to work.

2. Mix together the rye flour, buckwheat flour, wholemeal flour, salt and herbs in a large mixing bowl. Add the frothy yeast mixture and mix it in well to form a dough. Turn this out onto a floured board and knead it for about 15 minutes. Replace the dough in the mixing bowl and cover it with a clean cloth, then leave it in a warm place to rise until it has doubled in bulk.

3. Turn the dough back onto the floured board and knead again for another 2 or 3 minutes. Brush a 2 lb loaf tin with a little vegetable oil and place the dough in it. Let it rise again in the warmth until the bread reaches the top of the tin.

4. Bake at 400°F/200°C (Gas Mark 6) for the first 10 minutes. Then turn the heat down to 350°F/180°C (Gas Mark 4) and continue to bake for a further 35 minutes.

NUT BREADS

WALNUT COB LOAF
(Makes 1 large cob)

Imperial (Metric)	American
1 oz (25g) dried yeast	2½ tablespoonsful dried yeast
½ pint (¼ litre) warm water	1⅓ cupsful warm water
1 dessertspoonful clear honey	1 tablespoonful clear honey
1 lb (½ kilo) wholemeal flour	4 cupsful wholemeal flour
1 dessertspoonful sea salt	1 tablespoonful sea salt
3 oz (75g) walnut pieces	⅔ cupful walnut pieces

1. Dissolve the yeast in the warm water, add the honey and mix it in well. Leave the mixture to start bubbling in a warm spot.

2. Place the flour, salt and walnuts in a large mixing bowl and combine them well, then add the frothy yeast mixture and stir it in to form a dough.

3. Knead well on a floured surface for 10 to 15 minutes, then return the dough to the mixing bowl, cover it with a cloth and leave it in a warm place to double in size.

4. Knock back the dough to its former size for a few extra minutes, then knead it into a smooth, round ball. Put it onto a flat baking tray, cover it with a cloth and leave it to rise again.

5. Make a shallow cut across the top of the loaf to make the cob shape, then bake it at 400°F/200°C (Gas Mark 6) for 10 minutes. Reduce the heat to 350°F/180°C (Gas Mark 4) and continue to bake for a further 35 to 40 minutes.

ALMOND PLAIT-TOPPED BATON
(Makes 1 baton)

Imperial (Metric)	American
1 oz (25g) dried yeast	2½ tablespoonsful dried yeast
½ pint (¼ litre) warm water	1⅓ cupsful warm water
1 dessertspoonful clear honey	1 tablespoonful clear honey
1 dessertspoonful maple syrup	1 tablespoonful maple syrup
1 lb (½ kilo) wholemeal flour	4 cupsful wholemeal flour
1 dessertspoonful sea salt	1 tablespoonful sea salt
2 oz (50g) flaked almonds	½ cupful flaked almonds
1 oz (25g) whole blanched almonds	¼ cupful whole blanched almonds

1. Dissolve the yeast in the warm water, add the honey and maple syrup and stir well. Leave in a warm place to activate the yeast.

2. Put the flour, salt and flaked almonds into a large mixing bowl and mix them thoroughly. Pour the frothy yeast liquid into the flour and mix it in well to form a dough.

3. Knead the dough well on a floured surface for about 10 minutes. Return the dough to the bowl, cover it with a cloth and leave it to double in size in a warm place.

4. Knock back the dough for another 3 or 4 minutes, then break off a small piece of it and keep it on one side. Knead the larger piece of dough into a smooth, long baton shape, and place it on a flat baking tray.

5. Divide the smaller piece of dough into three equal pieces and roll each piece out into a long, thin strand, slightly longer than the baton. Join the three strands together at one end, plait them neatly and fix them together in the same way at the bottom.

6. Brush a line down the centre of the crust on the baton with some cold water and a pastry brush. Press the plait onto it and tuck the ends underneath the bottom of the loaf. Press the whole almonds firmly into the dough in an attractive pattern around the plait.

7. Cover the baton with a cloth and leave for the second rising in a warm place.

8. When the baton looks puffy and well risen, bake at 400°F/200°C (Gas Mark 6) for 10 minutes. Reduce the heat to 350°F/180°C (Gas Mark 4) and continue to bake for another 35 to 40 minutes.

PEANUT BUTTER BREAD
(Makes 1 large loaf)

Imperial (Metric)	American
2 oz (50g) fresh yeast	¼ cupful fresh yeast
1 dessertspoonful malt extract	1 tablespoonful malt extract
½ pint (¼ litre) warm water	1⅓ cupsful warm water
1 lb 2 oz (550g) wholemeal flour	4½ cupsful wholemeal flour
1½ dessertspoonsful sea salt	1 tablespoonful sea salt
3 dessertspoonsful peanut butter	3 tablespoonsful peanut butter
2 teaspoonsful Meaux mustard	2 teaspoonsful Meaux mustard

1. Place the yeast, malt extract and warm water in a bowl and mix them together with a fork until they are well blended. Leave in a warm place until the yeast starts to bubble.

2. Put the flour and salt together in a large mixing bowl and combine them well. When the yeast mixture is good and bubbly, carefully stir in the peanut butter and mustard. Use a whisk to help make the mixture smooth and evenly mixed. Pour this liquid into the flour and stir it in with a fork to form a dough.

3. When you have a smooth ball of dough, turn it out onto a well floured board and knead it gently for 10 to 15 minutes. Return the dough to the bowl and cover it with a cloth. Leave in a warm place for up to 45 minutes until the dough has doubled in bulk.

4. Knead the dough again for another few minutes and then shape it for the tin. Put it into a well oiled 2 lb loaf tin and leave it in a warm place, covered with a cloth, for another 20 minutes or so until the dough reaches the top of the tin.

5. Bake at 400°F/200°C (Gas Mark 6) for 15 minutes. Then turn the heat down to 350°F/180°C (Gas Mark 4) and bake for a further 40 minutes.

AMERICAN PEANUT COBURG
(Makes 1 large Coburg loaf)

Imperial (Metric)	American
1 oz (25g) dried yeast	2½ tablespoonsful dried yeast
½ pint (¼ litre) warm water	1⅓ cupsful warm water
1 dessertspoonful clear honey	1 tablespoonful clear honey
1 lb (½ kilo) wholemeal flour	4 cupsful wholemeal flour
1 dessertspoonful sesame salt	1 tablespoonful sesame salt
3 oz (75g) shelled, unsalted peanuts	½ cupful shelled, unsalted peanuts
A little beaten egg	A little beaten egg

1. Dissolve the yeast in the warm water and add the honey. Leave the mixture in a warm place to start bubbling.

2. Place the flour, sesame salt and peanuts in a large mixing bowl and stir them together.

3. Pour the frothy yeast mixture into the flour and mix them thoroughly to form a dough. Knead the dough well on a floured board for 10 to 15 minutes.

4. Return the dough to the bowl, cover it with a cloth and leave it in a warm spot to double in size.

5. Knock back the dough for another few minutes, then knead it into a round, smooth ball. Place the dough on a flat baking tray, cover it with a cloth and leave it in a warm place for the second rising.

6. When the dough has nearly risen enough, mark a cross on the top of the crust with a sharp knife. Leave it for a few more minutes in the warm for the cross to open.

7. Brush the surface of the crust all over with a little beaten egg, then bake the loaf at 400°F/200°C (Gas Mark 6) for 10 minutes. Then reduce the heat to 350°F/180°C (Gas Mark 4) and continue to bake for another 35 to 40 minutes on a middle shelf.

PINE KERNEL PLAIT
(Makes 1 large plait)

Imperial (Metric)	American
3 oz (75g) pine kernels	²/₃ cupful pine kernels
2 oz (50g) fresh yeast	¼ cupful fresh yeast
1 dessertspoonful clear honey	1 tablespoonful clear honey
½ pint (¼ litre) warm water	1¹/₃ cupsful warm water
1 lb (½ kilo) wholemeal flour	4 cupsful wholemeal flour
1 dessertspoonful sea salt	1 tablespoonful sea salt
A little beaten egg	A little beaten egg

1. Place the pine kernels in a dry frying pan and dry roast them over a fairly high heat, stirring constantly with a wooden spoon until the kernels are lightly and evenly browned.

2. Cream the yeast and the honey together with a fork in a small bowl. Add the warm water and stir it in well. Leave the mixture in a warm place to start frothing.

3. Place the flour, salt and pine kernels in a large mixing bowl and stir them together well. Add the frothy yeast mixture and stir to form a dough. Turn it out onto a well floured board and knead well for about 10 minutes. Return the dough to the bowl, cover with a cloth and leave in a warm place to double in size.

4. Knock back the dough for another few minutes and then divide the dough into three equal pieces. Roll each piece into a long, thin strand and join them together at one end, using a little cold water to make them stick together. Plait the three strands loosely and fix them together at the other end in the same way. Put the plait on a flat baking tray and brush the surface with some beaten egg.

5. Leave the plait in a warm place until it has risen well and looks puffy. Bake at 400°F/200°C (Gas Mark 6) for 10 minutes, then reduce the heat to 350°F/180°C (Gas Mark 4) and continue to bake for a further 10 minutes.

PISTACHIO NUT COTTAGE LOAF
(Makes 1 cottage loaf)

Imperial (Metric)	American
1 oz (25g) dried yeast	2½ tablespoonsful dried yeast
½ pint (¼ litre) warm water	1⅓ cupsful warm water
1 dessertspoonful clear honey	1 tablespoonful clear honey
4 oz (100g) pistachio nuts, roughly crushed	¾ cupful pistachio nuts, roughly crushed
1 dessertspoonful sea salt	1 tablespoonful sea salt
1 lb (½ kilo) wholemeal flour	4 cupsful wholemeal flour

1. Dissolve the yeast in the warm water and stir in the honey. Leave the mixture in a warm place until it becomes frothy.

2. Place the remaining ingredients in a large mixing bowl. Mix them together well and make a well in the centre.

3. Pour the yeast mixture into the well and mix it in to form a dough.

4. Knead the dough vigorously on a floured surface for about 15 minutes. Return the dough to the bowl, cover it with a cloth and keep it in the warm until doubled in size.

5. Knock back the dough for a few minutes, then divide it into two pieces, one twice as large as the other. Knead the larger piece into a smooth ball and place it on a flat baking tray. Knead the smaller piece in the same way until it is smooth and round, and then fix it in place on top of the other piece. Make a hole through the middle of both pieces with the floured handle of a wooden spoon.

6. Cover the loaf with a cloth and leave it in a warm spot until puffy and well risen. Bake at 400°F/200°C (Gas Mark 6) for 10 minutes, then reduce the heat to 350°F/180°C (Gas Mark 4) and continue to bake for a further 20 to 25 minutes.

PECAN NUT BATON
(Makes two 10 in. batons)

Imperial (Metric)	American
1 oz (25g) dried yeast	2½ tablespoonsful dried yeast
½ pint (¼ litre) warm water	1⅓ cupsful warm water
1 dessertspoonful clear honey	1 tablespoonful clear honey
1 dessertspoonful malt extract	1 tablespoonful malt extract
2 oz (50g) pecan nuts, roughly crushed	½ cupful pecan nuts, roughly crushed
1 dessertspoonful sea salt	1 tablespoonful sea salt
1 lb (½ kilo) wholemeal flour	4 cupsful wholemeal flour

1. Put the yeast into the warm water and stir it in well until dissolved. Stir in the honey and the malt extract and leave it in a warm place to start bubbling.

2. Place the remaining ingredients in a large mixing bowl and combine them well. Pour the bubbly yeast mixture into the flour and mix it in well to form a dough.

3. Knead the dough well on a floured board for about 15 minutes, then return it to the mixing bowl, cover it with a cloth and leave it in a warm spot to double in size.

4. Knock back the dough for another few minutes, then divide it into two equal pieces.

5. Knead each piece into a 10 in. long baton, slightly tapered at the ends, and place them on a flat baking tray. Slash the top of each baton crosswise in three or four places, cover them with a cloth and leave in the warm to rise again.

6. When the batons look puffy and well risen, bake them at 400°F/ 200°C (Gas Mark 6) for 10 minutes. Reduce the heat to 350°F/ 180°C (Gas Mark 4) and continue to bake on the lowest shelf for a further 10 to 15 minutes.

COCONUT LOAF
(Makes 1 large loaf)

Imperial (Metric)	American
1 oz (25g) dried yeast	2½ tablespoonsful dried yeast
1 dessertspoonful honey	1 tablespoonful honey
½ pint (¼ litre) warm milk	1⅓ cupsful warm milk
1 dessertspoonful sea salt	1 tablespoonful sea salt
4 oz (100g) desiccated coconut	1⅓ cupsful desiccated coconut
1 lb (½ kilo) wholemeal flour	4 cupsful wholemeal flour

1. Blend the yeast into the honey and add the warm milk. Stir well until the yeast dissolves completely, then put the mixture in a warm position until it starts to froth and bubble.

2. Place the remaining ingredients in a large mixing bowl and add the frothy yeast mixture. Mix thoroughly to form a dough.

3. Knead well for up to 15 minutes, using plenty of extra flour if you need to. Put the dough back into the bowl and cover it with a cloth, then leave in a warm place until it doubles in size.

4. Knock back the dough again for a further couple of minutes. Shape the loaf into a smooth oblong and put it into a well oiled, 2 lb loaf tin. Leave it in the warmth again for the second rising, until it reaches the top of the tin.

5. Bake at 400°F/200°C (Gas Mark 6) for 10 minutes, then turn the heat down to 350°F/180°C (Gas Mark4) and bake for a further 30 to 35 minutes.

SWEET CHESTNUT COB
(Makes 1 large cob)

Imperial (Metric)	American
2 oz (50g) fresh yeast	¼ cupful fresh yeast
1 dessertspoonful clear honey	1 tablespoonful clear honey
¼ pint (150ml) warm water	⅔ cupful warm water
1 lb 2 oz (550g) wholemeal flour	4½ cupsful wholemeal flour
1 teaspoonful sea salt	1 teaspoonful sea salt
⅓ pint (200ml) chestnut purée	¾ cupful chestnut paste
6 tablespoonsful warm milk	½ cupful warm milk

1. Cream the yeast and honey together in a small bowl. Add the warm water and stand the mixture in a warm place to start frothing.

2. Place the flour and salt in a large mixing bowl and combine them thoroughly.

3. Mix the chestnut *purée* and milk together until thoroughly blended, then add them to the frothy yeast liquid. Pour this into the flour and mix it in well to form a dough.

4. Turn the dough out onto a well floured board and knead it for 10 minutes or so until it feels more elastic. Return the dough to the bowl, cover it with a cloth and leave in a warm place until doubled in bulk.

5. Knock back the dough for another few minutes, then knead it into a smooth, round ball. Place the loaf on a flat baking tray, cover with a cloth and leave in a warm place until it looks puffy and well risen.

6. Bake at 400°F/200°C (Gas Mark 6) for 10 minutes. Reduce the heat to 350°F/180°C (Gas Mark 4) and bake for another 35 to 40 minutes.

FRUIT BREADS

APPLE AND RAISIN BLOOMER
(Makes 1 large bloomer)

Imperial (Metric)	American
1 oz (25g) dried yeast	2½ tablespoonsful dried yeast
½ pint (¼ litre) warm apple juice	1⅓ cupsful warm apple juice
1 dessertspoonful clear honey	1 tablespoonful clear honey
1 dessertspoonful malt extract	1 tablespoonful malt extract
1 lb (½ kilo) wholemeal flour	4 cupsful wholemeal flour
1 teaspoonful sea salt	1 teaspoonful sea salt
1 medium-sized eating apple, grated with the skin	1 medium-sized eating apple
2 oz (50g) raisins	⅓ cupful raisins

1. Add the yeast to the warm apple juice and stir until dissolved. Add the malt extract and honey and mix them in thoroughly. Put the mixture in a warm spot to activate the yeast.

2. Place the flour, salt, grated apple and raisins in a large mixing bowl and stir them together. Pour the frothy yeast liquid into the flour and mix it in well to form a dough.

3. Knead the dough vigorously for 10 to 15 minutes, then return it to the bowl, cover with a cloth and leave it in a warm place to double in size.

4. Knock back the dough again, and knead it into a 'bloomer' shape, a long oval, slightly narrower at the ends than in the

middle. Put this onto a flat baking tray and make several crosswise slashes along the length of the crust. Cover the loaf with a cloth and leave it to rise in a warm place.

5. When you judge the loaf to be puffy enough and well risen, bake it at 400°F/200°C (Gas Mark 6) for 10 minutes. Then reduce the heat to 350°F/180°C (Gas Mark 4) and continue to bake it for a further 35 to 40 minutes.

CIDER APPLE LOAF
(Makes 1 large loaf)

Imperial (Metric)	American
1 oz (25g) dried yeast	2½ tablespoonsful dried yeast
12 fl oz (350ml) dry cider, warm	1½ cupsful dry cider, warm
1 dessertspoonful honey	1 tablespoonful honey
6 oz (150g) eating apples, peeled and chopped	6 oz eating apples, peeled and chopped
1 lb 2 oz (550g) wholemeal flour	4½ cupsful wholemeal flour
1 dessertspoonful sea salt	1 tablespoonful sea salt

1. Dissolve the yeast in ½ pint (¼ litre) of the warmed cider and then add the honey. Mix them together well and leave in a warm place so that the yeast can start to work.

2. Put the remaining 4 tablespoonsful of cider into a small saucepan with the chopped apple, and simmer gently until the apple is quite soft. Pass this mixture through a fine sieve to make a *purée*.

3. Place the flour, and salt in a large mixing bowl, then add the apple *purée* and the frothy yeast mixture. Blend the mixture well to form a softish dough.

4. Knead the dough on a well floured surface for about 10 minutes. Put it back into the bowl and cover it with a clean tea-towel. Leave it in the warmth until it has doubled in size.

5. Knock back the dough for another few minutes, then shape it for the tin. Put it into a well oiled, 2 lb loaf tin and leave it in a warm place again until the top of the crust reaches the top of the tin.

6. Bake at 400°F/200°C (Gas Mark 6) for 10 minutes. Reduce the heat to 350°F/180°C (Gas Mark 4) and bake for a further 35 to 40 minutes.

CREAMY BANANA BREAD
(Makes 1 large and 1 small loaf)

Imperial (Metric)	American
2 oz (50g) fresh yeast	¼ cupful fresh yeast
1 dessertspoonful malt extract	1 tablespoonful malt extract
½ pint (¼ litre) warm water	1⅓ cupsful warm water
1 lb 6 oz (650g) wholemeal flour	5½ cupsful wholemeal flour
1 dessertspoonful sea salt	1 tablespoonsful sea salt
1½ medium-sized bananas	1½ medium-sized bananas
8 tablespoonsful double cream	⅔ cupful heavy cream

1. Put the yeast, malt extract and warm water together in a small bowl and mix well together with a fork. Let it stand in a warm place for about 10 minutes until the yeast starts to bubble.

2. Place the flour and salt in a large mixing bowl. Grate or mash the bananas and mix them into the flour, making sure they are evenly distributed. Make a well in the centre of this and pour the yeasty mixture into it.

3. Mix well to form a soft dough. Turn the dough out onto a well floured surface and knead it gently for about 10 minutes. Return it to the bowl and leave it somewhere warm to rise, for about 30 to 45 minutes.

4. When it has doubled in bulk, knead it again for a few minutes, then divide it into two pieces, one large and one small. Knead each piece into a smooth oblong and place the large piece in a well oiled 2 lb bread tin. Put the small piece into a well oiled 1 lb bread tin and place them in the warmth again to allow them to rise for the second time.

5. When the bread reaches the tops of the tins, bake at 400°F/200°C (Gas Mark 6) for 10 minutes. Then reduce the heat to 350°F/180°C (Gas Mark 4) and continue to bake for another 40 to 45 minutes.

ORANGE AND GINGER LOAF
(Makes 2 large loaves)

Imperial (Metric)	American
¾ pint (400ml) pure orange juice	2 cupsful pure orange juice
2 oz (50g) fresh yeast	¼ cupful fresh yeast
1 dessertspoonful honey	1 tablespoonful honey
2 lb (1 kilo) wholemeal flour	8 cupsful wholemeal flour
3 teaspoonsful ground ginger	3 teaspoonsful ground ginger
1 dessertspoonful sea salt	1 tablespoonful sea salt

1. Heat the orange juice to a lukewarm temperature and stir in the fresh yeast and honey. Blend them together well and leave the mixture somewhere warm for a few minutes until the yeast starts to bubble.

2. Place the flour, ground ginger and salt together in a large mixing bowl and combine them well. Make a well in the centre of the flour and pour the yeast mixture into it. Mix the liquid in, drawing the flour away from the sides of the bowl and into the centre. Mix to a stiff dough.

3. Knead the dough for about 10 minutes until it starts to feel more elastic. Put it back into the bowl and cover it with a clean cloth. Set it in the warmth and leave it for 1 to 1½ hours to rise.

4. Knock back the dough for another few minutes. Cut the dough into 2 equal pieces and knead each one into a smooth oblong shape to fit the tins.

5. Place each one in a well oiled 2 lb loaf tin and leave to rise again somewhere warm for another 30 to 45 minutes. When the loaves reach the tops of their tins, bake at 400°F/200°C (Gas Mark 6) for 10 minutes. Then reduce the heat to 350°F/180°C (Gas Mark 4) and continue to bake for another 40 minutes.

6. Remove the loaves from their tins and cool on a wire rack.

EGG AND LEMON HONEY LOAF
(Makes 1 large loaf)

Imperial (Metric)	American
2 oz (50g) fresh yeast	¼ cupful fresh yeast
4 dessertspoonsful clear honey	4 tablespoonsful clear honey
¼ pint (150ml) warm water	⅔ cupful warm water
3 large eggs, beaten	3 large eggs, beaten
1 lb 10 oz (800g) wholemeal flour	6½ cupsful wholemeal flour
1 teaspoonful sea salt	1 teaspoonful sea salt
3 tablespoonsful lemon juice	3½ tablespoonsful lemon juice

1. Cream the yeast into 1 dessertspoonful of the honey and mix in the warm water. Add the beaten eggs, stir well and leave the mixture in a warm place to start frothing.

2. Place the flour and salt in a large mixing bowl. Mix well, and when the yeast liquid looks good and frothy, pour the lemon juice and remaining honey into it, stirring well until dissolved. Pour it into the flour and mix well to form the dough.

3. Turn the dough out onto a well floured board and knead for 10 to 15 minutes, then return it to the bowl, cover it with a cloth and leave it in a warm place to double in bulk.

4. Knock back the dough again for another couple of minutes and then shape the loaf for the tin.

5. Place the loaf in a well oiled 2 lb loaf tin and leave it to rise again in a warm place. (Keep a careful eye on the dough at this stage, because it rises at an incredible rate due to the large amount of honey in it which activates the yeast.)

6. When the crust just reaches the top of the tin, bake the loaf at 400°F/200°C (Gas Mark 6) for 10 minutes. Reduce the heat to 350°F/180°C (Gas Mark 4) and continue to bake for a further 35 to 40 minutes.

LEMON BREAD
(Makes 1 large loaf)

Imperial (Metric)	American
1 dessertspoonful honey	1 tablespoonful honey
2 oz (50g) fresh yeast	¼ cupful fresh yeast
⅓ pint (200ml) warm water	¾ cupful warm water
1 lb (½ kilo) wholemeal flour	4 cupsful wholemeal flour
1 dessertspoonful sea salt	1 tablespoonful sea salt
4 dessertspoonsful lemon juice	4 tablespoonsful lemon juice

1. Cream the honey and the fresh yeast together with a fork and add the warm water. Combine them well and leave the mixture in the warmth to froth.

2. Place the flour and salt in a large mixing bowl and stir them together. When the yeast is sufficiently bubbly, mix the lemon juice into it, then add this mixture to the flour and work the ingredients to a soft dough.

3. Turn the dough out onto a floured board and knead for 15 minutes. Replace the dough in the bowl and cover it with a cloth. Leave it to rise for about 45 minutes in a warm place.

4. Turn the dough back out onto the floured board and knead it again for another few minutes. Shape it to fit the tin. Place it in a well oiled 2 lb loaf tin and set it in the warmth again for another 15 to 30 minutes until it rises to the top of the tin.

5. Bake at 400°F/200°C (Gas Mark 6) for 10 minutes, then reduce the heat to 350°F/180°C (Gas Mark 4) and continue to bake for another 30 to 40 minutes.

Note: This bread has an excellent, slightly tangy flavour, which in particular makes a very good salad/mayonnaise sandwich.

FRESH CHERRY LOAF
(Makes 1 large loaf)

Imperial (Metric)
2 oz (50g) fresh yeast
1 dessertspoonful honey
½ pint (¼ litre) warm water
½ lb (¼ kilo) fresh, ripe cherries,
stoned and chopped
1 teaspoonful sea salt
1½ (¾ kilo) wholemeal flour

American
¼ cupful fresh yeast
1 tablespoonful honey
1⅓ cupsful warm water
2 cupsful fresh, ripe cherries,
stoned and chopped
1 teaspoonful sea salt
6 cupsful wholemeal flour

1. Cream the yeast and the honey together in a small bowl using a fork. Add the warm water and leave the mixture in a warm place to start bubbling.

2. Place the remaining ingredients in a large mixing bowl and combine them well. Pour the bubbly yeast liquid into the flour and mix it in well to form a dough.

3. Turn the dough out onto a floured board and knead it lightly for 10 to 15 minutes. The cherries will gradually blend into the dough making it quite pink in colour. Return the dough to the bowl, cover it with a cloth and leave it in a warm place until it has doubled in size.

4. Knock back the dough for another couple of minutes and shape it for the tin. Place the loaf in a well oiled 2 lb tin and leave it to rise in a warm place.

5. When the dough reaches the top of the tin, bake at 400°F/ 200°C (Gas Mark 6) for 10 minutes, then reduce the heat to 350°F/180°C (Gas Mark 4) and bake for a further 35 to 40 minutes.

RASPBERRY BREAD WITH YOGURT
(Makes 1 large loaf)

Imperial (Metric)	American
½ pint (¼ litre) natural yogurt	1⅓ cupsful natural yogurt
2 oz (50g) fresh yeast	¼ cupful fresh yeast
3 dessertspoonsful honey	3 tablespoonsful honey
1½ lb (¾ kilo) wholemeal flour	6 cupsful wholemeal flour
1 teaspoonful sea salt	1 teaspoonful sea salt
½ lb (¼ kilo) fresh raspberries	2 cupsful fresh raspberries

1. Gently warm the yogurt in a saucepan until it is lukewarm and turns more liquid in consistency. Cream the fresh yeast and the honey together in a small bowl, then add the yogurt and stir it in well. Leave the mixture in a warm place to start bubbling.

2. Place the flour, salt and raspberries in a large mixing bowl and combine them. Pour the frothy yeast mixture into the flour and mix it in well to form a dough. Turn it out onto a floured surface and knead it lightly for 10 to 15 minutes. (The raspberries will gradually blend into the dough to make it quite pink.) Return the dough to the bowl, cover it with a cloth and leave it in a warm place to double in size.

3. Knock back the dough for another few minutes, then shape it for the tin. Place it in a well oiled 2 lb loaf tin and leave it in a warm place to rise again until the crust reaches the top of the tin.

4. Bake at 400°F/200°C (Gas Mark 6) for 10 minutes, then reduce the heat to 350°F/180°C (Gas Mark 4) and continue to bake for a further 35 to 40 minutes.

FRUIT-STUFFED PLAIT
(Makes 1 large plait)

Imperial (Metric)
2 oz (50g) fresh yeast
1 dessertspoonful clear honey
½ pint (¼ litre) warm milk
1 lb 2 oz (550g) wholemeal flour
1 teaspoonful sea salt
1 beaten egg
A little extra beaten egg

American
¼ cupful fresh yeast
1 tablespoonful clear honey
1⅓ cupful warm milk
4½ cupsful wholemeal flour
1 teaspoonful sea salt
1 beaten egg
A little extra beaten egg

Fruit filling:

Imperial (Metric)
4 oz (100g) currants
2 oz (50g) sultanas
2 oz (50g) raisins
2 oz (50g) mixed cut peel
1 dessertspoonful clear honey

American
⅔ cupful currants
⅓ cupful golden seedless raisins
⅓ cupful raisins
5 tablespoonsful mixed cut peel
1 tablespoonful clear honey

1. Cream the yeast into the honey and add the warm milk. Leave the mixture in a warm place for the yeast to start bubbling.

2. Place the flour and salt in a large mixing bowl and mix them together. Add the beaten egg to the frothy yeast mixture and then pour it into the flour, mixing well to form a dough.

3. Turn the dough out onto a floured board and knead well for about 10 minutes, using plenty of extra flour. Return the dough to the bowl, cover it with a cloth and leave it to double in size in a warm place.

4. While the dough is rising, make the fruit filling by mixing together the currants, sultanas, raisins, cut peel and honey in a small bowl.

5. Knock back the dough for a few minutes, then knead it into a rough rectangle shape. Roll the dough out quite thinly with a rolling pin, keeping the shape rectangular. Make ten slits in the dough, five on each side of the long side of the rectangle, as in diagram a). Spoon the fruit filling carefully down the centre, and fold the side pieces of dough over the fruit as shown in diagram b).

6. Place the loaf on a flat baking tray and brush the surface of the loaf all over with the extra beaten egg, then leave it to rise in a warm place.

7. When the loaf looks adequately risen and puffed up, bake it at 400°F/200°C (Gas Mark 6) for 10 minutes. Then reduce the heat to 350°F/180°C (Gas Mark 4) and continue to bake for a further 10 to 15 minutes.

a) Fruit Filling   b)

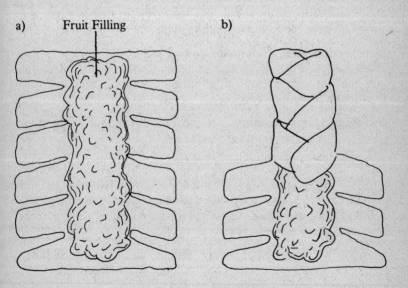

PINEAPPLE HONEY LOAF
(Makes 1 large loaf)

Imperial (Metric)	American
1 oz (25g) dried yeast	2½ tablespoonsful dried yeast
½ pint (¼ litre) warm pineapple juice	1⅓ cupsful warm pineapple juice
3 dessertspoonsful clear honey	3 tablespoonsful clear honey
1 lb 3 oz (575g) wholemeal flour	4¾ cupsful wholemeal flour
1 teaspoonful sea salt	1 teaspoonful sea salt
6 oz (150g) fresh pineapple, chopped (or pineapple tinned in its own juice)	6 oz fresh pineapple, chopped (or pineapple tinned in its own juice)

1. Dissolve the yeast in the warmed pineapple juice, and add the honey. Stir well and leave the mixture in a warm place for 10 to 15 minutes until the yeast starts frothing.

2. Put the flour, salt and chopped pineapple into a large mixing bowl and combine them well, making sure that each piece of pineapple is evenly coated with flour.

3. Pour the frothy yeast mixture into the flour and mix it in to form a dough. Turn the dough out onto a well floured board and knead it lightly for 10 to 15 minutes, using extra flour if the dough becomes too sticky.

4. Return the dough to the bowl, cover with a cloth and leave it in a warm place to double in size.

5. Knead the dough again for another few minutes, then shape it into a smooth oblong to fit your tin.

6. Place the dough in a well oiled 2 lb loaf tin, cover it with a cloth and leave in a warm place until the crust reaches the top of the tin.

7. Bake at 400°F/200°C (Gas Mark 6) for 10 minutes. Then reduce the heat to 350°F/180°C (Gas Mark 4) and bake for a further 35 to 40 minutes.

APRICOT NUT LOAF
(Makes 1 large loaf)

Imperial (Metric)	**American**
1 dessertspoonful honey	1 dessertspoonful honey
2 oz (50g) fresh yeast	¼ cupful fresh yeast
½ pint (¼ litre) warm water	1⅓ cupsful warm water
2 oz (50g) dried apricots	½ cupful dried apricots
2 oz (50g) hazelnuts, chopped	⅓ cupful hazelnuts, chopped
1 lb 2 oz (550g) wholemeal flour	4½ cupsful wholemeal flour
1 dessertspoonful sea salt	1 tablespoonful sea salt

1. Dissolve the honey and the fresh yeast in the warm water and make sure they are well blended with no lumps. Leave the mixture in a warm place until the yeast starts to work (about 10 to 15 minutes).

2. Simmer the apricots in plenty of boiling water until they are soft and thoroughly cooked. Drain and dry them on a clean tea-towel or kitchen paper, then chop them into small pieces.

3. Place the apricot pieces in a large mixing bowl together with the hazelnuts, flour and salt. Mix everything together well, making sure that all the pieces of apricot are individually coated in flour and remain separate.

4. Mix the yeasty liquid into the flour and work it in to form a dough. Knead the dough on a well floured board for 10 minutes or so, then put it back into the mixing bowl and leave it in the warmth to rise until it has doubled its size.

5. Knead the dough again for another couple of minutes, finally shaping it to fit the tin. Place it in a well oiled 2 lb loaf tin and keep it warm so that it can continue to rise to the top of the tin.

6. Bake at 400°F/200°C (Gas Mark 6) for 10 minutes, then lower the temperature to 350°F/180°C (Gas Mark 4) and bake for another 30 to 40 minutes.

MALT FRUIT LOAF
(Makes 1 large loaf)

Imperial (Metric)	American
1 oz (25g) butter	2½ tablespoonsful butter
1 tablespoonful molasses	1 tablespoonful molasses
1½ tablespoonsful malt extract	1½ tablespoonsful malt extract
1 lb (½ kilo) wholemeal flour	4 cupsful wholemeal flour
1 teaspoonful sea salt	1 teaspoonful sea salt
3 oz (75g) raisins	½ cupful raisins
1½ oz (40g) dried yeast	3½ tablespoonsful dried yeast
1 dessertspoonful honey	1 tablespoonful honey
¼ pint (150ml) warm water	⅔ cupful warm water
1 egg yolk mixed with	1 egg yolk mixed with
1 teaspoonful cold water	1 teaspoonful cold water

1. Melt the butter, molasses and malt extract together in a saucepan, but do not let the mixture boil. Leave to cool, stirring occasionally.

2. Put the flour, salt and raisins into a large mixing bowl and combine them well.

3. Mix the yeast and honey together and add the warm water, then leave the mixture somewhere warm to start bubbling.

4. When the yeast is ready, mix it into the flour, add the malt extract liquid and mix thoroughly. Shape the dough, which should be fairly stiff, into a ball and put it onto a lightly floured board.

5. Knead the dough for 10 to 15 minutes until it starts to feel more stretchy and pliable. Return the dough to the mixing bowl and place it in the warmth for up to 1½ hours while it rises. (Because of the fruit and extra malt extract and molasses, this bread is very slow rising, so give it plenty of time.)

6. When the dough has doubled in bulk, turn it back out onto a floured surface and continue to knead it for another few

minutes. Knead the dough into an oblong shape and put it into a well oiled 2 lb baking tin. Keep it in the warmth for another 45 minutes to 1 hour while it rises again.

7. When the dough reaches the tops of the tin, brush the surface with a generous layer of the egg yolk glaze. Bake at 300°F/ 150°C (Gas Mark 2) for 2 hours. (After the first 30 minutes, cover the top of the loaf loosely with silver foil for the remaining 1½ hours to prevent the top from burning while the inside is still cooking.)

DATE AND WALNUT LOAF
(Makes 1 large loaf)

Imperial (Metric)	American
2 oz (50g) walnuts	¼ cupful English walnuts
4 oz (100g) dates	¾ cupful dates
1 lb (½ kilo) wholemeal flour	4 cupsful wholemeal flour
1 teaspoonful sea salt	1 teaspoonful sea salt
1 egg	1 egg
¼ pint (150ml) milk	⅔ cupful milk
¼ pint (150ml) melted honey	⅔ cupful melted honey
2 teaspoonsful baking powder	2 teaspoonsful baking powder

1. Chop the walnuts and dates as finely as you can. Toss them in a little of the flour, mixing thoroughly so that the date pieces don't stick together. Add the salt and remaining flour.

2. Beat the egg into the milk, then make a well in the centre of the flour and pour the egg mixture into it. Add the melted honey and baking powder and gradually start to draw the flour away from the sides of the bowl into the liquid. When the two sets of ingredients are thoroughly mixed, turn the mixture out of the bowl and into a lightly oiled baking tin.

3. Bake at 350°F/180°C (Gas Mark 4) for 20 minutes. Then cover the loaf with a piece of silver foil and continue to bake at the same temperature for a further 50 minutes.

BREADS WITH VEGETABLES

SAVOURY MUSHROOM LOAF
(Makes 1 large loaf)

Imperial (Metric)	American
2 oz (50g) fresh yeast	¼ cupful fresh yeast
1 dessertspoonful clear honey	1 tablespoonful clear honey
½ pint (¼ litre) warm water	1⅓ cupsful warm water
1 lb (½ kilo) wholemeal flour	4 cupsful wholemeal flour
1 dessertspoonful sea salt	1 tablespoonful sea salt
4 oz (100g) button mushrooms	2 cupsful button mushrooms
1 dessertspoonful mushroom ketchup	1 tablespoonful mushroom ketchup

1. Cream the fresh yeast and honey together and add the warm water. Stir the mixture well and leave it in a warm place to start frothing.

2. Put the flour and salt into a large mixing bowl. Chop the mushrooms very finely, add them to the flour and mix them in thoroughly.

3. Stir the mushroom ketchup into the frothy yeast mixture and add it to the flour, mixing well to form a dough.

4. Knead the dough on a very well floured board (as this dough can be sticky) for 10 to 15 minutes, until it feels more elastic and stretchy. Return the dough to the bowl, cover it with a cloth and leave it to rise in a warm place.

5. Knock back the dough for another 2 or 3 minutes, then shape the loaf and place it in a well oiled 2 lb loaf tin. Cover it with a cloth and leave it to rise in a warm place.

6. When the dough is nearing the top of the tin, bake it at 400°F/ 200°C (Gas Mark 6) for 10 minutes. (This dough rises very quickly so keep an eye on it and don't overprove it.) Reduce the heat to 350°F/180°C (Gas Mark 4) and continue to bake the loaf for a further 35 to 40 minutes.

SWEET CORN LOAF
(Makes 1 large loaf)

Imperial (Metric)	American
2 oz (50g) fresh yeast	¼ cupful fresh yeast
1 dessertspoonful clear honey	1 tablespoonful clear honey
½ pint (¼ litre) warm water	1⅓ cupsful warm water
1 lb 2 oz (550g) wholemeal flour	4½ cupsful wholemeal flour
1 dessertspoonful sea salt	1 dessertspoonful sea salt
6 oz 6150g) sweet corn kernels	1 cupful sweet corn kernels

1. Place the yeast and honey in a small bowl and cream them together with a fork. Add the warm water and leave the mixture in a warm place to start frothing.

2. Put the flour, salt and sweet corn into a large mixing bowl and mix them together well.

3. Pour the frothy yeast liquid into the flour and mix it well to form a dough. Turn it out onto a well floured board and knead it for 10 to 15 minutes. Return the dough to the bowl, cover it with a cloth and leave it to double in size in a warm place.

4. Knock back the dough for a further 2 or 3 minutes, then shape it for your tin.

5. Place it in a well oiled 2 lb loaf tin, cover it with a cloth and leave it to rise again in a warm place until it reaches the top of the tin.

6. Bake the loaf at 400°F/200°C (Gas Mark 6) for 10 minutes, then reduce the heat to 350°F/180°C (Gas Mark 4) and continue to bake for a further 35 to 40 minutes.

SAVOURY TOMATO LOAF
(Makes 1 large loaf)

Imperial (Metric)	American
2 oz (50g) fresh yeast	¼ cupful fresh yeast
1 dessertspoonful honey	1 tablespoonful honey
½ pint (¼ litre) warm water	1⅓ cupsful warm water
4 tablespoonsful tomato purée	⅓ cupful tomato paste
1 lb 2 oz (550g) wholemeal flour	4½ cupsful wholemeal flour
1 dessertspoonful sea salt	1 tablespoonful sea salt

This makes a fairly sticky dough, so use plenty of extra flour for kneading. The loaf keeps very well and seems to improve in flavour after a day or so, unlike most other breads. Also, the lovely colour and delicious flavour of this bread makes it a perfect candidate for open sandwiches.

1. Place the fresh yeast, honey and warm water in a small bowl and blend them well. When the yeast is bubbly, stir in the tomato *purée* and mix well.

2. Put the flour and salt into a large mixing bowl, pour in the yeast mixture, and stir well to form a dough.

3. Knead the dough on a floured board for 10 minutes or so until it starts to feel more elastic. Return the dough to the mixing bowl and cover it with a cloth, then leave it somewhere warm for about 30 minutes until it is twice its original size.

4. Using plenty of flour, knead it again for another few minutes, then shape the dough into a rounded oblong and put it in a well oiled 2 lb loaf tin. Cover the loaf with a cloth and leave it in the warmth again until the dough reaches the top of the tin.

5. Bake at 400°F/200°C (Gas Mark 6) for the first 10 minutes, then lower the heat to 350°F/180°C (Gas Mark 4) for a further 35 to 40 minutes.

FARMHOUSE ONION PLAIT
(Makes 1 large plait)

Imperial (Metric)	American
½ oz (15g) dried onions	1 tablespoonful dried onions
1 oz (25g) dried yeast	2½ tablespoonsful dried yeast
¼ pint (150ml) warm water	⅔ cupful warm water
¼ pint (150ml) warm milk	⅔ cupful warm milk
1 dessertspoonful clear honey	1 tablespoonful clear honey
1 lb (½ kilo) wholemeal flour	4 cupsful wholemeal flour
1 dessertspoonful onion salt	1 tablespoonful onion salt
2 teaspoonsful wholegrain mustard	2 teaspoonsful wholegrain mustard

1. Soak the dried onions in some boiling water for 5 minutes, then drain and dry them on kitchen paper.

2. Mix the dried yeast into the warm water, stirring it until dissolved. Add the warm milk and honey and stir thoroughly, then leave the mixture in the warmth for the yeast to start bubbling.

3. Put the flour and onion salt into a large mixing bowl and mix them together. Add the soaked, dried onion and mix it in well.

4. Mix the mustard into the yeast liquid and pour it into the flour, mixing to form a dough.

5. Knead the dough vigorously for about 10 minutes until it feels more elastic, then put it back into the bowl, cover it with a cloth and leave it to double in size in a warm place.

6. Knock back the dough for a few more minutes, then divide it into three equal pieces. Roll each piece into a long strand and join the three strands together at the top, fixing the ends with a little cold water to make them stick. Plait the strands together loosely, and secure them at the other end in the same way. Place the loaf carefully on a flat baking tray.

7. Cover the dough with a cloth and leave it in a warm place for the second rising. When the plait looks puffy and risen, bake it at

400°F/200°C (Gas Mark 6) for 10 minutes, then reduce the heat to 350°F/180°C (Gas Mark 4) and continue to bake on a low shelf for a further 20 minutes.

CARROT AND APPLE LOAF
(Makes 1 large loaf)

Imperial (Metric)	American
1 oz (25g) dried yeast	2½ tablespoonsful dried yeast
1 dessertspoonful clear honey	1 tablespoonful clear honey
½ pint (¼ litre) warm water	1⅓ cupsful warm water
1 large carrot	1 large carrot
1 medium-sized cooking apple	1 medium-sized cooking apple
14 oz (400g) wholemeal flour	3½ cupsful wholemeal flour
2 oz (50g) rye flour	½ cupful rye flour
1 teaspoonful sea salt	1 teaspoonful sea salt

1. Mix the yeast, honey and warm water together and leave the mixture in a warm spot to activate the yeast.

2. Grate the carrot and the apple into a large mixing bowl, then add the two sorts of flour and the salt and mix well.

3. Add the frothy yeast mixture and mix it in well to form a dough. Turn the dough out onto a well floured board and knead it for 10 to 15 minutes.

4. Return the dough to the bowl, cover it with a cloth and leave it to rise in a warm place until doubled in bulk.

5. Knock back the dough again for another couple of minutes, then shape it for your tin. Place it in a well oiled, large loaf tin, cover it with a cloth and leave it to rise again in a warm place.

6. When the dough reaches the top of the tin, bake it at 400°F/200°C (Gas Mark 6) for 10 minutes. Reduce the heat to 350°F/180°C (Gas Mark 4) and continue to bake for a further 35 to 40 minutes.

RED PEPPER AND ONION LOAF
(Makes 1 large loaf)

Imperial (Metric)	American
3 oz (75g) red pepper	3 oz red pepper
4 oz (100g) onion	4 oz onion
1 lb 4 oz (600g) wholemeal flour	5 cupsful wholemeal flour
1½ dessertspoonsful sea salt	1 tablespoonful sea salt
1 teaspoonful paprika pepper	1 teaspoonful paprika pepper
2 oz (50g) fresh yeast	¼ cupful fresh yeast
1 dessertspoonful honey	1 tablespoonful honey
½ pint (¼ litre) warm water	1⅓ cupsful warm water

1. Chop the red pepper and the onion as finely as you can and place them in a large mixing bowl. Add the flour, salt and paprika pepper and mix them together well.

2. Blend the yeast, honey and warm water together in a small bowl and leave the mixture in a warm position until it starts to bubble.

3. Add the yeast mixture to the flour and blend the two sets of ingredients with a fork, then mix with the hands until the dough is formed.

4. Knead the dough vigorously on a floured surface for about 10 minutes, then put it back in the bowl, cover it with a cloth and leave it in a warm place until it has risen to twice its original size.

5. Knead the dough again for another few minutes. Shape the loaf and place it in a well oiled 2 lb baking tin, then leave it to rise again for another 15 to 30 minutes until it reaches the top of the tin.

6. Bake at 400°F/200°C (Gas Mark 6) for 10 minutes, then reduce the heat to 350°F/180°C (Gas Mark 4) and bake for a further 40 to 45 minutes.

POTATO BREAD
(Makes 1 large loaf)

Imperial (Metric)	American
1 oz (25g) dried yeast	2½ tablespoonsful dried yeast
½ pint (¼ litre) warm water	1⅓ cupsful warm water
1 dessertspoonful malt extract	1 tablespoonful malt extract
1 teaspoonful ground nutmeg	1 teaspoonful ground nutmeg
1½ dessertspoonsful sea salt	1 tablespoonful sea salt
1 lb 2 oz (550g) wholemeal flour	4½ cupsful wholemeal flour
4 oz (100g) raw potato	4 oz raw potato
2 dessertspoonsful natural yogurt	2 tablespoonsful natural yogurt

1. Mix the yeast, warm water and malt extract together in a small bowl. Set the mixture aside in the warmth until it starts to froth and bubble.

2. Place all the other dry ingredients in a large mixing bowl and combine them well. Make a well in the centre of the flour mixture and pour the yeast mixture into it. Add the yogurt and blend it in well until a dough is formed.

3. Knead the dough for about 10 to 15 minutes on a well floured board until it starts to feel more elastic. Put it back into the bowl and cover it with a clean tea-towel, then leave it in the warmth for about 45 minutes until it has doubled in size.

4. Knock back the dough until it feels elastic again (2 or 3 minutes). Place it in a well oiled 2 lb loaf tin and cover it with a cloth, then leave in a warm place again until the crust of the loaf reaches the top of the tin.

5. Bake at 400°F/200°C (Gas Mark 6) for the first 10 minutes, then reduce the heat to 350°F/200°C (Gas Mark 4) and bake for a further 40 to 45 minutes.

SWEET POTATO BLOOMER
(Makes 1 large bloomer)

Imperial (Metric)	American
1 oz (25g) dried yeast	2¹/₂ tablespoonsful dried yeast
¹/₂ pint (¹/₄ litre) warm water	1¹/₃ cupsful warm water
1 dessertspoonful clear honey	1 tablespoonful clear honey
1 lb (¹/₂ kilo) wholemeal flour	4 cupsful wholemeal flour
1 dessertspoonful sea salt	1 tablespoonful sea salt
10 oz (300g) peeled sweet potato or yam	10 oz peeled sweet potato or yam
A little beaten egg	A little beaten egg

1. Put the yeast, warm water and honey into a small bowl, mix them well and leave the mixture in a warm place to start bubbling.

2. Place the flour and salt in a large mixing bowl and mix them together.

3. Chop the sweet potato into small pieces and boil it in water until soft and mushy, then mash it with a fork and add it to the flour, mixing well to avoid any lumps forming.

4. Add the frothy yeast mixture and mix it in well to form a dough. Knead the dough well for 10 to 15 minutes until it is smooth and elastic, using extra flour if it seems too sticky. Return the dough to the bowl, cover it with a cloth and leave it in a warm place to double in size.

5. Knock back the dough for another minute or so and then knead it into a smooth oblong shape. Place it on a flat baking tray, cover it with a cloth and leave it to rise in a warm place.

6. When the loaf looks well risen, make four or five slanted slashes in the crust and brush it with the beaten egg.

7. Bake at 400°F/200°C (Gas Mark 6) for 10 minutes, then reduce the heat to 350°F/180°C (Gas Mark 4) and continue to bake for a further 20 to 25 minutes.

CHICK PEA LOAF
(Makes 1 large loaf)

Imperial (Metric)	American
4 oz (100g) chick pea flour	1 cupful chick pea flour
14 oz (400g) wholemeal flour	3½ cupsful wholemeal flour
2 oz (50g) wheatgerm	½ cupful wheatgerm
2 dessertspoonsful sea salt	2 tablespoonsful sea salt
2 oz (50g) fresh yeast	¼ cupful fresh yeast
1 dessertspoonful clear honey	1 tablespoonful clear honey
½ pint (¼ litre) warm water	1⅓ cupsful warm water

1. Sieve the chick pea flour and place it in a large mixing bowl. Add the wholemeal flour, wheatgerm and salt and mix them thoroughly.

2. Cream the yeast into the honey until it is quite dissolved. Add the warm water and blend it in, then place the mixture in a warm spot and leave it to start working.

3. When the yeast mixture is frothy, pour it into the flour and mix it in with a fork to form a fairly stiff dough. Turn this out onto a floured board and knead until it starts to feel more elastic.

4. Put the dough back into the bowl and cover it with a cloth. Leave it somewhere warm for 30 minutes or so and then return it to the floured board. Continue to knead for about another 3 minutes.

5. Oil a 2 lb loaf tin and shape the dough to fit it. Place the dough in the tin and press the edges down all around it so that the loaf is slightly higher in the centre. Leave it in the warmth until the dough reaches the top of the tin.

6. Bake at 400°F/200°C (Gas Mark 6) for the first 10 minutes, then lower the heat to 350°F/180°C (Gas Mark 4) for a further 40 to 45 minutes.

NUTTY SOYA BLOOMER LOAF
(Makes 1 large bloomer)

Imperial (Metric)	American
2½ oz (65g) soya grits	⅓ cupful soya grits
1 dessertspoonful clear honey	1 tablespoonful clear honey
2 oz (50g) fresh yeast	¼ cupful fresh yeast
½ pint (¼ litre) warm water	1⅓ cupsful warm water
1 lb 4 oz (600g) wholemeal flour	5 cupsful wholemeal flour
1 dessertspoonful sea salt	1 tablespoonful sea salt
A little beaten egg	A little beaten egg

1. Put 2 oz (50g) of the soya grits into a small bowl and pour ½ pint (¼ litre) of boiling water over the top. (Leave the other ½ oz (15g) of soya grits dry.) Leave the grits to soak for 5 minutes or so, then press all the water out of them through a sieve.

2. Cream the honey and fresh yeast together in another small bowl, then add the warm water and stir well. Leave the mixture in a warm place to activate the yeast.

3. Put the flour, salt and soaked soya grits into a large mixing bowl and mix them together well. Pour the frothy yeast mixture into the flour and mix it in to form a dough.

4. Turn the dough out onto a well floured board and knead it for 10 to 15 minutes. Return the dough to the bowl, cover it with a cloth and leave it in a warm place to double in size.

5. Knock back the dough for another few minutes, then shape it into a smooth, oblong, bloomer shape, and place it on a flat baking tray. Make four or five slits across the top of the crust, spaced evenly apart.

6. Brush the top of the crust with the beaten egg and sprinkle the remaining ½ oz (15g) of dry soya grits over the top.

7. Leave the dough to rise again in a warm place until the bloomer looks puffy. Bake at 400°F/200°C (Gas Mark 6) for 10 minutes, then reduce the heat to 350°F/180°C (Gas Mark 4) and continue to bake for another 15 to 20 minutes.

CHEESE BREADS

CURD CHEESE MILK LOAF
(Makes 1 large loaf)

Imperial (Metric)	American
½ oz (15g) dried yeast	1 tablespoonful dried yeast
½ pint (¼ litre) warm milk	1⅓ cupsful warm milk
1 dessertspoonful clear honey	1 tablespoonful clear honey
1 lb 2 oz (550g) wholemeal flour	4½ cupsful wholemeal flour
1 teaspoonful sea salt	1 teaspoonful sea salt
½ lb (¼ kilo) curd cheese	1 cupful curd cheese
A little beaten egg	A little beaten egg

1. Combine the dried yeast, warm milk and honey in a small bowl and leave the mixture in a warm place until the yeast starts bubbling.

2. Place the flour and salt in a large mixing bowl and mix them thoroughly.

3. Whisk the curd cheese into the frothy yeast liquid and pour it into the flour, mixing until a dough is formed.

4. Knead the dough well on a floured board for 10 to 15 minutes, then return it to the bowl, cover it with a cloth and leave it in a warm place until doubled in size.

5. Knock back the dough for another couple of minutes, then shape the loaf for the tin. Place it in a lightly oiled, large loaf tin, cover it with a cloth, and leave it in a warm place until the crust reaches the top of the tin.

6. Brush the top of the loaf with the beaten egg and bake it at 400°F/200°C (Gas Mark 6) for 10 minutes. Reduce the heat to 350°F/180°C (Gas Mark 4) and continue to bake for a further 30 to 35 minutes.

SOFT CHEESE HERB LOAF
(Makes 1 large loaf)

Imperial (Metric)
7 oz (200g) low-fat soft cheese
¼ pint (150ml) warm water
2 oz (50g) fresh yeast
1 dessertspoonful malt extract
2 dessertspoonsful finely chopped
  fresh parsley
2 dessertspoonsful finely chopped
  fresh sage
1 lb (½ kilo) wholemeal flour
1½ dessertspoonsful sea salt

American
¾-1 cupful low-fat soft cheese
⅔ cupful warm water
¼ cupful fresh yeast
1 tablespoonful malt extract
2 tablespoonsful finely chopped
  fresh parsley
2 tablespoonsful finely chopped
  fresh sage
4 cupsful wholemeal flour
1 tablespoonful sea salt

1. Mix the soft cheese into the warm water and mix it to a creamy consistency.

2. Cream the yeast into the malt extract and add it to the cheese mixture, then leave this somewhere warm for the yeast to develop.

3. Place all the remaining ingredients in a large mixing bowl and mix them together thoroughly. Add the yeasty cheese mixture and stir it in with a fork. Then knead the mixture with the hands, pressing the mixture against the sides of the bowl until it forms a dough.

4. Put the dough onto a floured surface and knead it gently for about 10 minutes, then return it to the bowl and cover it with a cloth. Place the dough in a warm place and leave it to rise for about 45 minutes or until it is twice its original size.

5. Return the dough to the floured surface and knead it for another few minutes. Shape the dough into a smooth oblong.

6. Put the dough into a well oiled 2 lb loaf tin and leave it to rise again. When it reaches the top of the tin, bake it at 400°F/200°C (Gas Mark 6) for the first 10 minutes, then reduce the heat to 350°F/180°C (Gas Mark 4) and continue to bake it for a further 30 to 35 minutes.

CREAM CHEESE LOAF WITH CHIVES
(Makes 1 large loaf)

Imperial (Metric)	American
1 oz (25g) dried yeast	2½ tablespoonsful dried yeast
⅓ pint (200ml) warm water	¾ cupful warm water
1 dessertspoonful malt extract	1 tablespoonful malt extract
1 lb (½ kilo) wholemeal flour	4 cupsful wholemeal flour
1 dessertspoonful onion salt	1 tablespoonful onion salt
2 dessertspoonsful finely chopped fresh chives	2 tablespoonsful finely chopped fresh chives
6 oz (150g) cream cheese	¾ cupful cream cheese
4 dessertspoonsful milk	⅓ cupful milk

1. Dissolve the yeast in the warm water and then add the malt extract, stirring it in well until it has all quite dissolved. Leave the mixture in a warm place until the yeast starts to froth.

2. Put the flour, salt and chopped chives into a large mixing bowl and combine them well.

3. When the yeast is frothy, mix in the cream cheese and milk with a fork or a whisk until the mixture is quite smooth and creamy.

4. Pour the liquid into the flour and mix it to a soft dough.

5. Turn the dough out onto a floured board and knead it for about 10 minutes until it is smooth and quite elastic. Return the dough to the bowl, cover it with a cloth and leave it in a warm place to rise.

6. Knock back the dough for a few more minutes and then shape it for the tin.

7. Place the dough in a well oiled 2 lb loaf tin, cover it with a cloth and set it in a warm place for the second rising. When the dough reaches the top of the tin, bake it at 400°F/200°C (Gas Mark 6) for 10 minutes, then reduce the heat to 350°F/180°C (Gas Mark 4) and continue to bake for a further 35 to 40 minutes.

CHEESE AND CELERY BREAD
(Makes 2 large loaves)

This cheesy bread is especially good toasted. It has a fairly crumbly texture, so it is a good idea to let it cool completely before cutting it.

Imperial (Metric)	American
1 oz (25g) dried yeast	2½ tablespoonsful dried yeast
1 dessertspoonful honey	1 tablespoonful honey
¾ pint (400ml) warm water	2 cupsful warm water
2 oz (50g) celery	2 oz celery
4 oz (100g) Cheddar cheese, grated	1 cupful grated Cheddar cheese
1½ lb (¾ kilo) wholemeal flour	6 cupsful wholemeal flour
2 teaspoonsful sea salt	2 teaspoonsful sea salt

1. Cream the yeast and honey together and add the warm water. Leave the mixture covered in a warm place so that the yeast can start to work.

2. Chop the celery as finely as you can and put it in a large mixing bowl, then add the cheese to the celery.

3. Add the flour and salt and mix well, then pour in the warm water and mix to a soft dough.

4. Turn the dough out onto a floured board and knead it for about 10 minutes, adding a little extra flour if the dough becomes too sticky. Put the dough back into the mixing bowl and set it aside in a warm place to rise.

5. When the dough has doubled in bulk, turn it out onto the floured board again and knead it for a further 2 or 3 minutes.

6. Put the shaped loaf into a well oiled tin and let it rise again until the dough reaches the top of the tin.

7. Bake at 400°F/200°C (Gas Mark 6) for the first 10 minutes, then turn the heat down to 350°F/180°C (Gas Mark 4) and continue to bake for another 40 minutes or until the crust is golden brown.

ALFALFA CHEESE LOAF
(Makes 1 large loaf)

Imperial (Metric)	American
2 oz (50g) fresh yeast	¼ cupful fresh yeast
1 dessertspoonful honey	1 tablespoonful honey
½ pint (¼ litre) warm water	1⅓ cupful warm water
1 lb 2 oz (550g) wholemeal flour	4½ cupful wholemeal flour
1 dessertspoonful sea salt	1 tablespoonful sea salt
1 oz (25g) alfalfa sprouts	½ cupful alfalfa sprouts
3 oz (75g) Cheddar cheese, grated	¾ cupful grated Cheddar cheese

1. Put the fresh yeast, honey and warm water into a bowl and combine them well. Set the mixture aside in the warmth until the yeast starts to bubble.

2. Put the flour and salt into a large mixing bowl, chop the alfalfa sprouts very finely and add them to the flour, then mix in the cheese.

3. Make a well in the centre of the flour, pour the yeasty liquid into it and mix it in with a fork to form a smooth dough.

4. Turn the dough out onto a well floured board and knead it for 10 to 15 minutes until the dough appears more elastic. Put it back into the mixing bowl and place it in the warmth, covered with a clean cloth, until it doubles in size.

5. Turn the dough back out onto the floured board and knead it for another couple of minutes, then shape it for the tin. Place the dough in a well oiled tin and leave it in a warm place to continue to rise.

6. When the dough reaches the top of the tin, bake it at 400°F/200°C (Gas Mark 6) for the first 10 minutes. Then turn the heat down to 350°F/180°C (Gas Mark 4) and continue to bake it for another 30 to 40 minutes until the crust is golden brown.

STILTON BROWN BREAD
(Makes 1 large loaf)

Imperial (Metric)	American
2 oz (50g) fresh yeast	¼ cupful fresh yeast
1 dessertspoonful honey	1 tablespoonful honey
½ pint (¼ litre) warm water	1⅓ cupsful warm water
4 oz (100g) ripe Stilton cheese, grated	1 cupful grated ripe Stilton cheese
1 lb 2 oz (550g) wholemeal flour	4½ cupsful wholemeal flour
1½ dessertspoonsful sea salt	1 tablespoonful sea salt
3 dessertspoonsful grated Parmesan cheese	3 tablespoonsful grated Parmesan cheese

1. Mix the yeast, honey and warm water together in a small bowl and leave it somewhere warm to activate the yeast.

2. Place the Stilton cheese in a large mixing bowl, add the flour, salt and grated Parmesan cheese and mix them in thoroughly.

3. Add the frothy yeast mixture and mix it in well to form a soft dough. Turn the dough out onto a floured surface and knead it gently for about 10 minutes. Return the dough to the bowl, cover it with a cloth, and set it aside in the warmth to double in size.

4. Knead the dough again for another few minutes and then shape it for the tin. Place it in a well oiled 2 lb loaf tin and keep it in the warm until the dough reaches the top of the tin.

5. Bake at 400°F/200°C (Gas Mark 6) for 10 minutes, then reduce the heat to 350°F/180°C (Gas Mark 4) and continue to bake it for another 35 minutes.

HERB, SPICE AND
SEED BREADS

SAVOURY PARSLEY LOAF
(Makes 1 large loaf)

Imperial (Metric)	American
2 oz (50g) fresh yeast	¼ cupful fresh yeast
1 dessertspoonful honey	1 tablespoonful honey
½ pint (¼ litre) warm water	1⅓ cupsful warm water
1 lb 2 oz (550g) wholemeal flour	4½ cupsful wholemeal flour
2 dessertspoonsful sesame salt	2 tablespoonsful sesame salt
4 dessertspoonsful finely chopped fresh parsley	4 tablespoonsful finely chopped fresh parsley
A little vegetable oil	A little vegetable oil

1. Cream the yeast and honey together in a small bowl and add the warm water. Stand this mixture in the warmth for about 10 minutes until the yeast starts to bubble.

2. Mix the flour, sesame salt and chopped parsley together in a large mixing bowl. Stir in the yeast liquid and mix it in well to form a soft dough.

3. Turn the dough out onto a floured surface and knead it vigorously for 10 to 15 minutes until the dough starts to feel more elastic and pliable. Put the dough back into the bowl and leave it in a warm place, covered with a clean cloth, for about 45 minutes or until it has doubled in size.

4. Knock back the dough for another few minutes and shape it for the tin. Place it in a well oiled 2 lb loaf tin and set it aside in the warmth to rise again. When it reaches the top of the tin, brush it with the vegetable oil.

5. Bake at 400°F/200°C (Gas Mark 6) for the first 10 minutes, then turn the heat down to 350°F/180°C (Gas Mark 4) for another 40 minutes until the crust is golden brown and the loaf sounds hollow when tapped underneath.

Note: This recipe makes a pleasant-flavoured loaf which rises well and has a springy texture. It is especially good toasted and spread with herb or garlic butter.

GARLIC AND SAGE GARLAND
(Makes 1 garland — enough to serve 4 to 6)

Imperial (Metric)	American
1 oz (25g) fresh yeast	2½ tablespoonsful fresh yeast
1 teaspoonful honey	1 teaspoonful honey
¼ pint (150ml) warm water	⅔ cupful warm water
9 oz (250g) wholemeal flour	1¾ cupsful wholemeal flour
1 teaspoonful sea salt	1 teaspoonful sea salt
3 dessertspoonsful finely chopped fresh sage	3 tablespoonsful finely chopped fresh sage
3 cloves garlic	3 cloves garlic

1. Cream the yeast and honey together and add the warm water. Leave the mixture in a warm place for 10 minutes or so until the yeast starts to work.

2. In a large mixing bowl combine the flour, salt and finely chopped sage leaves. Crush the garlic cloves in a garlic press and add them to the flour, mixing well.

3. Make a well in the centre of the flour and pour the yeast liquid into it. Mix it in well with a fork, then use the hands to press the mixture until it knits together in a soft dough.

4. Turn the dough out onto a board, lightly sprinkle it with wholemeal flour and then knead it vigorously for about 10 to 15 minutes, then put it back in the mixing bowl and cover it with a clean cloth. Place the dough somewhere warm and leave it to rise until it has doubled in bulk.

5. Turn the dough out again and sprinkle it with a little extra wholemeal flour. Continue to knead it for another couple of minutes until it feels soft and pliable again, adding more flour as necessary.

6. Roll the dough out into a long sausage shape, about 16 inches long. Place it on a well oiled, flat baking tray and curve it around in a circle. Join the two ends together to form a ring and set it in the warmth again to rise for another 15 minutes or until it has doubled in size again.

7.   Bake at 400°F/200°C (Gas Mark 6) for 15 minutes.

Note: For the best results, serve it hot, straight from the oven, with butter.

SEMOLINA SPICE BREAD
(Makes 1 large loaf)

Imperial (Metric)	American
1 dessertspoonful honey	1 tablespoonful honey
2 oz (50g) fresh yeast	¼ cupful fresh yeast
⅓ pint (200ml) warm water	¾ cupful warm water
¾ lb (350g) wholemeal flour	3 cupsful wholemeal flour
2 oz (50g) wholewheat semolina	⅓ cupful wholewheat semolina
1 dessertspoonful sea salt	1 tablespoonful sea salt
2 teaspoonsful ground cummin	2 teaspoonsful ground cummin

1.   Dissolve the honey and fresh yeast in the warm water and set this aside somewhere warm to allow the yeast to start working.

2.   Meanwhile put the flour, wholewheat semolina, salt and ground cummin into a large bowl and mix them together well. When the yeast is bubbling well, mix it into the flour and gently blend them together until the dough has formed.

3.   Sprinkle some wholemeal flour onto a board and turn the dough out onto it. Knead it well for about 15 minutes, then return the dough to the bowl and set it somewhere warm away from draughts for about 45 minutes until the dough has doubled in bulk.

4.   Knock back the dough briefly and then shape the loaf for the tin. Place it in a well oiled 2 lb loaf tin and keep it in the warm so that it can continue to rise.

5.   When the dough reaches the top of the tin, bake it at 400°F/200°C (Gas Mark 6) for 10 minutes. Then reduce the heat to 350°F/180°C (Gas Mark 4) for another 30 to 40 minutes.

SESAME MILK ROLL
(Makes 1 large rolled loaf)

Imperial (Metric)	American
1 oz (25g) dried yeast	2½ tablespoonsful dried yeast
½ pint (¼ litre) warm milk	1⅓ cupsful warm milk
1 dessertspoonful clear honey	1 tablespoonful clear honey
1 lb (¼ kilo) wholemeal flour	4 cupsful wholemeal flour
1 dessertspoonful sea salt	1 tablespoonful sea salt
1 oz (25g) sesame seeds	2½ tablespoonsful sesame seeds

1. Dissolve the yeast in the warm milk and add the honey. Stir the mixture well and leave it in a warm place to start bubbling.

2. Put the flour and salt into a large mixing bowl and combine them well.

3. Pour the frothy yeast mixture into the flour and mix it in well to form a dough.

4. Turn the dough out onto a floured board and knead it well for 15 minutes or so. Return the dough to the bowl, cover it with a cloth and leave it in a warm place to double in size.

5. Knock back the dough for another few minutes, then roll it out into a large, thin rectangle, making the short side the same length as your tin. Brush the surface of the dough with a little cold water, and sprinkle the sesame seeds evenly over the rectangle.

6. Roll the dough up, Swiss roll fashion, sealing the bottom with cold water. Place it in a well oiled 2 lb baking tin, with the seal on the bottom, cover it with a cloth and leave it in a warm place to rise.

7. When the top of the loaf reaches the top of the tin, bake the dough at 400°F/200°C (Gas Mark 6) for 10 minutes. Reduce the heat to 350°F/180°C (Gas Mark 4) and continue to bake for another 35 to 40 minutes.

SESAME BRAN BREAD
(Makes 1 large loaf)

Imperial (Metric)	American
1½ oz (40g) fresh yeast	3½ tablespoonsful fresh yeast
1 dessertspoonful honey	1 tablespoonful honey
⅔ pint (350ml) warm water	1½ cupful warm water
1 lb (½ kilo) wholemeal flour	4 cupsful wholemeal flour
3 oz (75g) coarse wheat bran	¾ cupful coarse wheat bran
1 teaspoonful sea salt	1 teaspoonful sea salt
½ oz (15g) sesame seeds	1 tablespoonful sesame seeds

1. Cream the yeast and honey and add the warm water, then set the mixture aside in a warm place to froth.

2. Put the flour, bran, salt and sesame seeds into a large bowl and mix them well.

3. Pour the yeast mixture into the flour and mix it to a fairly stiff dough. Turn the dough out and knead it for about 10 minutes, then return it to the mixing bowl, cover with a clean cloth and leave it in a warm place for an hour or so until it has doubled in bulk.

4. Turn the dough out again onto a floured board and knead it for another 2 or 3 minutes until smooth again. Shape it into a smooth-topped rectangle and place it in an oiled tin, then leave it to rise for another 30 minutes or so until it reaches the top of the tin.

5. Bake at 400°F/200°C (Gas Mark 6) for the first 10 minutes, then turn down the heat and bake it for a further 30 to 35 minutes.

6. Leave the loaf to cool on a wire rack.

BLACK OLIVE AND SESAME LATTICE LOAF
(Makes 1 large, round loaf)

Imperial (Metric)	American
2 oz (50g) fresh yeast	¼ cupful fresh yeast
1 dessertspoonful honey	1 tablespoonful honey
½ pint (¼ litre) warm water	1⅓ cupsful warm water
1 lb (½ kilo) wholemeal flour	4 cupsful wholemeal flour
1 teaspoonful sesame salt	1 teaspoonful sesame salt
16 whole black olives	16 whole black olives
A little milk	A little milk
1 dessertspoonful sesame seeds	1 tablespoonful sesame seeds

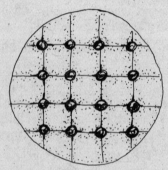

1. Cream the yeast and honey in a small bowl using a fork. Stir in the warm water and leave the mixture in a warm place to start bubbling.

2. Put the flour and salt into a large mixing bowl and stir them together. Add the frothy yeast liquid and mix it in well to form a dough.

3. Turn the dough out onto a floured board and knead it well for about 10 minutes. Return the dough to the bowl, cover it with a cloth and leave it to double in bulk in a warm place.

4. Knock back the dough for another few minutes, then knead it into a smooth, round ball. Roll the ball out into a large, flat circle using a rolling pin.

5. Make eight shallow cuts in the dough in a lattice shape (as shown in the diagram). Press a whole black olive firmly into each place where the lines cross. Place the dough on a flat baking tray and brush the surface with the milk. Sprinkle the sesame seeds over the top as evenly as possible, and leave the dough to rise in a warm spot.

6. When the dough looks well risen, bake it at 400°F/200°C (Gas Mark 6) for 10 minutes, then reduce the heat to 350°F/180°C (Gas Mark 4) and continue to bake it for a further 10 to 15 minutes.

POPPY SEED CROWN LOAF
(Makes 1 crown loaf)

Imperial (Metric)	American
1 oz (25g) dried yeast	2½ tablespoonsful dried yeast
½ pint (¼ litre) warm water	1⅓ cupsful warm water
1 dessertspoonful clear honey	1 tablespoonful clear honey
1 lb (½ kilo) wholemeal flour	4 cupsful wholemeal flour
1 teaspoonful sea salt	1 teaspoonful sea salt
A little milk	A little milk
1 dessertspoonful poppy seeds	1 tablespoonful poppy seeds

1. Dissolve the yeast in the warm water, add the honey and leave the mixture in a warm place to start frothing.

2. Put the flour and salt into a large mixing bowl and mix them thoroughly. Add the yeast mixture and mix it in well to form a dough.

3. Knead the dough well for 10 to 15 minutes on a floured board, then roll it into a ball and place back in the bowl. Cover it with a cloth and leave it to rise in a warm spot.

4. Knock back the dough for an extra few minutes, then divide it into seven equal pieces and roll each piece into a smooth ball. Oil a round sandwich tin and place six of the rolls around the outside in a ring. Place the seventh roll in the middle.

5. Cover the dough with a cloth and let rise again in a warm place. When the loaf looks puffy and well risen, brush the surface with the milk and sprinkle the poppy seeds over the top.

6. Bake at 400°F/200°C (Gas Mark 6) for 10 minutes, then reduce the heat to 350°F/180°C (Gas Mark 4) and continue to bake it for a further 10 to 15 minutes.

SUNFLOWER LOAF
(Makes 1 large loaf)

Imperial (Metric)	American
2 oz (50g) fresh yeast	¼ cupful fresh yeast
1 dessertspoonful honey	1 tablespoonful honey
½ pint (¼ litre) warm water	1⅓ cupsful warm water
2 dessertspoonsful sea salt	2 tablespoonsful sea salt
1 lb (½ kilo) wholemeal flour	4 cupsful wholemeal flour
6 oz (150g) sunflower seeds	1½ cupsful sunflower seeds

1. Cream the yeast and honey together in a small bowl and add the warm water, blending these three ingredients together thoroughly. Leave the mixture in a warm place so that the yeast can start to work.

2. Place all the dry ingredients in a large mixing bowl and mix them together carefully. Pour in the frothy yeast mixture and stir it in with a fork. Gradually shape the dough into a smooth ball with your hands until there is no loose flour left at the bottom of the bowl.

3. Place the dough on a well floured surface and knead it until you feel the dough becoming more pliable and stretchy (about 10 minutes). Return the dough to the bowl and cover it with a cloth, then leave it somewhere warm so that it can rise. (It should have doubled in size after about 30 to 45 minutes.)

4. Knead the dough again for another 5 minutes and then shape it into an oblong. Place it in a well oiled 2 lb loaf tin and leave it in the warmth for another 30 minutes or so until the dough reaches the top of the tin.

5. Bake at 400°F/200°C (Gas Mark 6) for 15 minutes, then reduce the heat to 350°F/180°C (Gas Mark 4) and continue to bake for another 35 to 40 minutes.

PLAITED EGG BREAD WITH POPPY SEEDS
(Makes 1 large plait)

Imperial (Metric)	American
2 tablespoonsful honey	2½ tablespoonsful honey
2 oz (50g) fresh yeast	¼ cupful fresh yeast
¼ pint (150ml) warm milk	⅔ cupful warm milk
2 eggs	2 eggs
1 tablespoonful vegetable oil	1 tablespoonful vegetable oil
1 lb 2 oz (550g) wholemeal flour	4½ cupsful wholemeal flour
2 teaspoonsful sea salt	2 teaspoonsful sea salt
2 teaspoonsful honey, mixed with a few drops of hot water	2 teaspoonsful honey, mixed with a few drops of hot water
1 tablespoonful poppy seeds	1 tablespoonful poppy seeds

1. Cream the honey and the yeast together until no lumps are left, then mix in the warm milk. Leave the mixture in the warmth until the yeast starts to bubble.

2. Put the eggs and the vegetable oil in another small bowl and beat them with a fork.

3. Place the flour and salt in a large mixing bowl and mix them thoroughly. Add the yeast liquid and the beaten eggs and mix them in well, then press the ingredients together until a soft dough is formed.

4. Knead the dough on a floured board for 10 to 15 minutes until the dough becomes more pliable, then put it back into the mixing bowl, cover it with a cloth and leave it in a warm, draught-free place until it doubles in size.

5. Turn the dough back out onto the floured board and knead it again for another few minutes, then divide the dough into three equal pieces. Roll each piece out into a long, thin strand and fix the tops of the three strands together, using a little water to help stick them together.

6. Plait the three pieces together loosely and fix the ends together at the bottom. Place the dough on a lightly floured, flat baking tray and cover it with a clean tea-towel. Leave the dough in the warmth for another 30 minutes or so until the plait looks puffed up and well risen.

7. Brush the whole of the top crust with the honey and water mixture, then sprinkle the poppy seeds over the top.

8. Bake at 400°F/200°C (Gas Mark 6) for 10 minutes, then cover the plait with a piece of silver foil and turn the temperature down to 350°F/180°C (Gas Mark 4). Continue to bake the loaf for another 15 minutes.

PUMPKIN SEED AND SULTANA LOAF
(Makes 1 large loaf)

Imperial (Metric)	American
1¾ oz (45g) dried yeast	3½ tablespoonsful dried yeast
½ pint (¼ litre) warm water	1⅓ cupsful warm water
1 dessertspoonful honey	1 tablespoonful honey
2 oz (50g) sultanas	⅓ cupful golden seedless raisins
2 oz (50g) whole pumpkin seeds	½ cupful whole pumpkin seeds
1 lb 4 oz (600g) wholemeal flour	5 cupsful wholemeal flour
1 dessertspoonful celery salt	1 tablespoonful celery salt

1. Dissolve the yeast in the warm water and stir in the honey. Leave the mixture in a warm place to allow the yeast to start bubbling.

2. Put the remaining dry ingredients together in a large mixing bowl and combine them well. Pour the frothy yeast mixture into the centre of the dry ingredients and mix it in with a fork, then knead the dough for about 10 to 15 minutes.

3. Return the dough to the mixing bowl, cover it with a clean cloth and leave it in a warm place until the dough has doubled in bulk.

4. Knead the dough again for another couple of minutes, then shape it to fit the tin. Oil the tin well and place the dough in it, then cover it again with a clean cloth and set it in the warmth for another 30 minutes or so until the dough reaches the top of the tin.

5. Bake at 400°F/200°C (Gas Mark 6) for 10 minutes, then reduce the heat to 350°F/180°C (Gas Mark 4) and continue to bake for another 30 to 35 minutes. Turn the loaf out of the tin and leave it to cool on a wire rack. Eat this bread while it is still fresh (within two days).

BREADS USING
SPECIAL INGREDIENTS

COFFEE BREAD
(Makes 1 large loaf)

Imperial (Metric)	American
2 oz (50g) fresh yeast	¼ cupful fresh yeast
1 dessertspoonful malt extract	1 tablespoonful malt extract
½ pint (¼ litre) strong black coffee	1⅓ cupsful strong black coffee
1 lb 2 oz (550g) wholemeal flour	4½ cupsful wholemeal flour
1½ dessertspoonsful sea salt	1 tablespoonful sea salt

1. Cream the yeast into the malt extract and add the warm coffee, blending them thoroughly. Leave the mixture in a warm place to allow the yeast to start working.

2. Put the remaining ingredients into a large mixing bowl and combine them well. Add the frothy yeast mixture and mix it in to form a soft dough. Turn this out onto a floured board and knead it for up to 10 minutes.

3. Return the dough to the mixing bowl and cover it with a clean cloth. Set the dough in a warm position and leave it to rise, until it has doubled in bulk.

4. Knock back the dough and shape it into an oblong. Put it in a well oiled 2 lb loaf tin and press the dough well into the corners of the tin. Leave the loaf somewhere warm to rise again and when it nears the top of the tin, put it in a moderate oven at 350°F/180°C (Gas Mark 4) for 45 minutes.

CREAMY GOAT'S MILK RING
(Makes 1 large ring)

Imperial (Metric)	American
1 oz (25g) dried yeast	2½ tablespoonsful dried yeast
¼ pint (150ml) warm goat's milk	⅔ cupful warm goat's milk
1 dessertspoonful clear honey	1 tablespoonful clear honey
1 lb (½ kilo) wholemeal flour	4 cupsful wholemeal flour
1 dessertspoonful sea salt	1 tablespoonful sea salt
¼ pint (150ml) double cream	⅔ cupful heavy cream

1. Dissolve the yeast in the warm milk and then add the honey. Leave the mixture in a warm spot to activate the yeast.

2. Put the flour and salt in a large mixing bowl and combine them well.

3. Stir the cream into the frothy yeast liquid and add it to the flour. Mix it in well to form a dough, adding a little extra goat's milk if the dough is too stiff.

4. Knead the dough vigorously on a floured board for 15 minutes, then return it to the mixing bowl, cover it with a cloth and leave it to rise in a warm place until doubled in bulk.

5. Knock back the dough for another couple of minutes, then knead it into a long stick.

6. Place the stick on a flat baking tray, curving it round to form a ring. Fix the two ends together with a little cold water, cover it with a cloth and leave it in a warm place until doubled in size again.

7. Bake at 400°F/200°C (Gas Mark 6) for 10 minutes, then reduce the heat to 350°F/180°C (Gas Mark 4) and continue to bake for a further 10 to 15 minutes.

ENRICHED TOFU LOAF
(Makes 1 large loaf)

Imperial (Metric)	American
1 oz (25g) dried yeast	2½ tablespoonsful dried yeast
½ pint (¼ litre) warm water	1⅓ cupsful warm water
1 dessertspoonful honey	1 tablespoonful honey
5 oz (125g) tofu (soya bean curd)	¾ cupful tofu (soya bean curd)
2 dessertspoonsful milk	2 tablespoonsful milk
1 lb 4 oz (600g) wholemeal flour	5 cupsful wholemeal flour
1 dessertspoonful sea salt	1 tablespoonful sea salt

1. Dissolve the yeast in the warm water, stirring it until it completely dissolves. Add the honey and stir it in well, then leave the mixture in a warm place until it starts to froth.

2. Whisk the tofu and the milk into the yeasty mixture and blend them thoroughly.

3. Put the flour and salt into a large mixing bowl, add the frothy yeast mixture and mix it in well to form a dough.

4. Knead the dough vigorously for about 10 minutes and when it begins to feel more elastic and stretchy, roll it into a ball and place it back in the mixing bowl. Cover the dough with a cloth and leave it in the warmth until it has doubled in size.

5. Turn the dough back out of the bowl and knead it again briefly until it returns to its former size. Knead it into a smooth loaf shape to fit your tin and place it in the oiled tin covered with the cloth again.

6. When the dough almost reaches the top of the tin, bake it at 400°F/200°C (Gas Mark 6) for 10 minutes, then turn down the heat to 350°F/180°C (Gas Mark 4) and bake it for a further 15 minutes. Cover the loaf with silver foil at this stage and continue to bake it for another 15 minutes.

MUESLI COB LOAF
(Makes 1 large loaf)

Imperial (Metric)	American
1 dessertspoonful clear honey	1 tablespoonful clear honey
2 oz (50g) fresh yeast	¼ cupful fresh yeast
½ pint (¼ litre) warm water	1⅓ cupsful warm water
1 lb (½ kilo) wholemeal flour	4 cupsful wholemeal flour
1 teaspoonful sea salt	1 teaspoonful sea salt
4 oz (100g) muesli	1 cupful muesli
A little beaten egg	A little beaten egg

1. Cream the honey and yeast together in a small bowl, add the warm water, stir it in well and leave the mixture in a warm place to start bubbling.

2. Put the flour, salt and muesli into a large mixing bowl and combine them well.

3. Pour the frothy yeast mixture into the flour and mix it in well to form a dough.

4. Turn the dough out onto a well floured board and knead it for 10 to 15 minutes, using extra wholemeal flour if the dough becomes too sticky. Return the dough to the bowl, cover it with a cloth and leave it to rise in a warm place until it has doubled in size.

5. Knock back the dough for another few minutes, then knead it into a smooth, round ball. Place it on a flat baking tray, cover it with a cloth and leave it to rise again in a warm place.

6. When the loaf has risen well and looks puffed up, brush the surface with the beaten egg.

7. Bake at 400°F/200°C (Gas Mark 6) for 10 minutes, then reduce the heat to 350°F/180°C (Gas Mark 4) and continue to bake for a further 20 minutes.

MAPLE AND HONEY SWEET LOAF
(Makes 1 large loaf)

Imperial (Metric)	American
1 oz (25g) dried yeast	2½ tablespoonsful dried yeast
⅓ pint (200ml) warm water	¾ cupful warm water
2 dessertspoonsful clear honey	2 tablespoonsful clear honey
1 lb (½ kilo) wholemeal flour	4 cupsful wholemeal flour
1 teaspoonful sea salt	1 teaspoonful sea salt
1 beaten egg	1 beaten egg
3 tablespoonsful maple syrup	2½ tablespoonsful maple syrup

1. Dissolve the yeast in the warm water and add the honey, then leave the mixture in a warm place to activate the yeast.

2. Put the flour and salt in a large mixing bowl and combine them well.

3. Stir the beaten egg and the maple syrup into the frothy yeast mixture, add this to the flour and mix it in well to form a dough.

4. Turn out the dough onto a lightly floured surface and knead it vigorously for 10 to 15 minutes. Return the dough to the bowl and cover it with a cloth, then leave it in a warm place to double in bulk.

5. Knock back the dough for another couple of minutes and shape it into a rounded rectangle.

6. Place the loaf in a well oiled 2 lb baking tin and cover it with a cloth, then leave it in a warm place again until the dough reaches the top of the tin.

7. Bake the loaf at 400°F/200°C (Gas Mark 6) for 10 minutes, then reduce the heat to 350°F/180°C (Gas Mark 4) and cover the top of the loaf with silver foil as it tends to brown very quickly. Continue to bake for another 35 to 40 minutes.

CHUTNEY WHOLEMEAL COTTAGE LOAF
(Makes 1 large cottage loaf)

Imperial (Metric)	**American**
1 dessertspoonful clear honey	1 tablespoonful clear honey
½ pint (¼ litre) warm water	1⅓ cupsful warm water
1 oz (25g) dried yeast	2½ tablespoonsful dried yeast
1 lb (½ kilo) wholemeal flour	4 cupsful wholemeal flour
1 teaspoonful sea salt	1 teaspoonful sea salt
3 dessertspoonsful vegetable or fruit chutney	3 tablespoonsful vegetable or fruit chutney
A little beaten egg	A little beaten egg

1. Put the honey, warm water and dried yeast together in a small bowl, blend them well and leave the mixture in a warm place to activate the yeast.

2. Put the flour and salt together in a large mixing bowl and combine them well. Mix the chutney into the yeast liquid and pour it into the flour, mixing it in well to form a dough.

3. Knead the dough for 10 to 15 minutes on a well floured board, return it to the bowl, cover it with a cloth and leave it to double in size in a warm place.

4. Knock back the dough for a few more minutes and then divide it into two pieces, one large and one small. Knead the large piece into a smooth, round ball and place it in a large, round oven-proof dish or cake tin. Knead the small piece into a smooth, round ball and set it neatly on top of the large piece. Make a hole through the centre of both pieces with the floured handle of a wooden spoon. Cover the dough with a cloth and leave it to rise in a warm place until puffy.

5. Brush the surface of the crust with the beaten egg and bake the loaf at 400°F/200°C (Gas Mark 6) for 10 minutes. Reduce the heat to 350°F/180°C (Gas Mark 4) and continue to bake it for another 20 to 25 minutes.

WHEATGERM LOAF
(Makes 1 large loaf)

This wheatgerm loaf is creamy and delicious with a good texture. The flavour is quite sweet and it also slices well.

Imperial (Metric)	American
1½ oz (40g) fresh yeast	3½ tablespoonsful fresh yeast
1 dessertspoonful honey	1 tablespoonful honey
⅔ pint (350ml) warm water	1½ cupsful warm water
1 lb 4 oz (600g) wholemeal flour	5 cupsful wholemeal flour
1 teaspoonful sea salt	1 teaspoonful sea salt
3 oz (75g) wheatgerm	¾ cupful wheatgerm
A little beaten egg	A little beaten egg

1. Cream the yeast and honey together in a small bowl, add the warm water and leave the mixture in the warmth until it works up a good froth.

2. Sieve the flour and salt into a large mixing bowl and mix in the wheatgerm.

3. Stir the frothy yeast mixture into the flour and mix it in well to form a soft dough. Knead this on a well floured board for about 10 minutes, then return the dough to the mixing bowl, cover it with a cloth and leave it in a warm place to double in size.

4. Knock back the dough for 2 or 3 minutes on a floured board until it forms a smooth ball. Press this into a well oiled bread tin and leave it to rise to the top of the tin.

5. Brush the surface of the loaf with the beaten egg and place it in a hot oven at 400°F/200°C (Gas Mark 6) for 10 minutes. Reduce the heat to 350°F/180°C (Gas Mark 4) and continue to bake for a further 20 to 25 minutes until the crust is golden brown and the loaf is cooked.

HIGH BRAN LOAF
(Makes 1 large loaf)

Imperial (Metric)	American
1 oz (25g) dried yeast	2½ tablespoonsful dried yeast
1 dessertspoonful malt extract	1 tablespoonful malt extract
½ pint (¼ litre) warm water	1⅓ cupsful warm water
1 lb (½ kilo) wholemeal flour	4 cupsful wholemeal flour
1 teaspoonful sesame salt	1 teaspoonful sesame salt
1 oz (25g) wheatgerm	¼ cupful wheatgerm
4 oz (100g) wheat bran	1 cupful wheat bran
6 tablespoonsful milk	½ cupful milk

1. Mix the yeast, malt extract and warm water together in a small bowl, then leave the mixture in a warm place to start bubbling.

2. Put the flour, sesame salt, wheatgerm and bran into a large mixing bowl and combine them thoroughly.

3. Pour the milk into the frothy yeast mixture and mix it with the flour, stirring it in well to form a dough.

4. Turn the dough out onto a well floured board and knead it for about 10 minutes. Return the dough to the bowl, cover it with a cloth and leave it to rise in a warm place until doubled in bulk.

5. Knock back the dough for a few more minutes, then shape it to fit your tin. Place the dough in a lightly oiled, large loaf tin, cover it with a cloth and leave it in the warmth again until the dough reaches the top of the tin.

6. Bake at 400°F/200°C (Gas Mark 6) for 10 minutes. Reduce the heat to 350°F/180°C (Gas Mark 4) and continue to bake for a further 35 to 40 minutes.

MALTED WHEAT FLAKE BREAD
(Makes 1 large loaf)

Imperial (Metric)	American
1 dessertspoonful honey	1 tablespoonful honey
2 oz (50g) fresh yeast	¼ cupful fresh yeast
½ pint (¼ litre) warm water	1⅓ cupsful warm water
1 lb 2 oz (550g) wholemeal flour	4½ cupsful wholemeal flour
2 oz (50g) malted wheat flakes	1¼ cupsful malted wheat flakes
1 dessertspoonful sea salt	1 tablespoonful sea salt
1 teaspoonful molasses	1 teaspoonful molasses

1. Dissolve the honey and the fresh yeast in the warm water and set the mixture aside somewhere warm to activate the yeast.

2. Put the flour, malted wheat flakes and salt together in a large mixing bowl and stir them well. When the yeasty liquid is frothy, add the molasses to it and stir well to make sure that it all dissolves. Mix this liquid into the flour and work it all in to form a dough.

3. Turn the dough out onto a floured board and knead it gently for about 15 minutes. Return the dough to the mixing bowl and leave it in the warmth for approximately 45 minutes until it has doubled in size.

4. Knock back the dough for another couple of minutes and then shape it for the tin. Place it in a well oiled 2 lb loaf tin and leave it in the warmth for the second rising.

5. When it reaches the top of the tin bake the loaf at 400°F/200°C (Gas Mark 6) for 10 minutes, then reduce the heat to 350°F/180°C (Gas Mark 4) for another 30 minutes. Turn the bread out of the tin and leave it to cool on a wire rack.

BULGUR BREAD
(Makes 1 large loaf)

If you have trouble getting a wholemeal loaf to rise sufficiently, then this recipe is for you. The addition of the soaked bulgur has the effect of making a softer, more pliable loaf with the result that it rises well. In fact, this dough rises so well and so quickly that you need to keep a watchful eye on it to make sure it doesn't overprove!

Imperial (Metric)	American
3 oz (75g) dry bulgur (cracked wheat)	½ cupful bulgur (cracked wheat)
¾ pint (400ml) boiling water	2 cupsful boiling water
1 lb 2 oz (550g) wholemeal flour	4½ cupsful wholemeal flour
1 dessertspoonful sea salt	1 tablespoonful sea salt
2 oz (50g) fresh yeast	¼ cupful fresh yeast
1 dessertspoonful malt extract	1 tablespoonful malt extract
½ pint (¼ litre) warm water	1⅓ cupsful warm water

1. Soak the bulgur in the boiling water for about 30 minutes. When cool, drain it in a sieve and press out any excess water with your hands. Put the bulgur in a large mixing bowl and add the flour and salt, combining them thoroughly.

2. Put the yeast, malt extract and warm water together in a small bowl and blend them with a fork. Leave the mixture for about 10 minutes until it is bubbly.

3. Add the yeast mixture to the flour and form it into a ball. Knead the dough gently for 10 minutes or so, then put it back into the bowl and leave it in a warm place until it has doubled in size. Return the dough to the floured board and knead it again for another few minutes.

4. Shape the dough into a rectangle to fit a well oiled 2 lb loaf tin. Place the dough in the tin and let it rise to the rim.

5. Bake at 400°F/200°C (Gas Mark 6) for 15 minutes, then reduce the heat to 350°F/180°C (Gas Mark 4) and continue to bake for a further 40 to 50 minutes.

ROLLS, FARLS, BAPS AND FLATBREADS

BUTTERMILK ROLLS
(Makes 8)

Imperial (Metric)	American
1 dessertspoonful clear honey	1 tablespoonful clear honey
½ pint (¼ litre) warm buttermilk	1⅓ cupsful warm buttermilk
1 oz (25g) dried yeast	2½ tablespoonsful dried yeast
1 lb (½ kilo) wholemeal flour	4 cupsful wholemeal flour
1 teaspoonful sea salt	1 teaspoonful sea salt
3 oz (75g) butter	⅓ cupful butter
A little beaten egg	A little beaten egg
1 dessertspoonful poppy seeds	1 tablespoonful poppy seeds

1. Mix the honey into the warmed buttermilk and add the dried yeast, stirring it in well until dissolved. Put the mixture in a warm place to activate the yeast.

2. Put the flour and salt into a large mixing bowl and mix them together well. Rub the butter into the flour lightly.

3. Pour the yeast liquid into the flour and mix it in well to form a dough. Knead the dough well on a floured board for 10 to 15 minutes, then return it to the bowl, cover it with a cloth and put it in a warm place until it has doubled in size. (This might take longer than usual because this dough is a slow riser, so give it plenty of time.)

4. Knock back the dough for a few more minutes and then divide it into eight equal pieces. Knead each piece into a smooth, round ball and place them on a flat baking tray, spaced evenly apart. Cover them with a cloth and leave them in a warm place until well risen. (This may take over an hour.)

5. Brush the tops of the rolls with the beaten egg and sprinkle the poppy seeds over the top.

6. Bake at 400°F/200°C (Gas Mark 6) for 10 to 15 minutes.

SAVOURY CASHEW NUT ROLLS
(Makes 12)

Imperial (Metric)	American
2 oz (50g) fresh yeast	¼ cupful fresh yeast
1 dessertspoonful clear honey	1 tablespoonful clear honey
½ pint (¼ litre) warm water	1⅓ cupsful warm water
1 lb (½ kilo) wholemeal flour	4 cupsful wholemeal flour
1 teaspoonful sea salt	1 teaspoonful sea salt
4 oz (100g) roasted, salted cashew nuts	¾ cupful roasted, salted cashew nuts

1. Cream the yeast and honey in a small bowl and add the warm water. Stir the mixture well and leave it in a warm place to activate the yeast.

2. Put the flour, salt and cashew nuts into a large mixing bowl and stir them together.

3. Pour the frothy yeast mixture into the flour and mix it in well to form a dough.

4. Turn the dough onto a well floured board and knead it for 10 to 15 minutes. Return the dough to the bowl, cover it with a cloth and leave it to double in size in a warm place.

5. Knock back the dough for another couple of minutes and then divide it into 12 equal pieces. Knead each piece into a smooth, round roll and place them on a flat baking tray.

6. Leave the dough in a warm place to rise again until the rolls look puffy.

7. Bake at 400°F/200°C (Gas Mark 6) for 10 minutes.

ALMOND ROLLS
(Makes 12 rolls)

Imperial (Metric)	American
2 oz (50g) fresh yeast	¼ cupful fresh yeast
1 dessertspoonful honey	1 tablespoonful honey
½ pint (¼ litre) warm water	1⅓ cupsful warm water
1 lb 2 oz (550g) wholemeal flour	4½ cupsful wholemeal flour
2 oz (50g) ground almonds	½ cupful ground almonds
1½ dessertspoonsful sea salt	1 tablespoonful sea salt
12 whole almonds	12 whole almonds

1. Put the yeast, honey and warm water together into a small bowl and cream them until the liquid is quite smooth. Leave the mixture in a warm position until it starts to froth.

2. Put the flour, ground almonds and salt into a large mixing bowl and mix them together well. Add the yeasty liquid and stir it in well. Gradually draw the flour from around the edges of the bowl into the liquid in the centre until a dough is formed.

3. Turn the dough out onto a well floured board and knead it until the dough feels more elastic and pliable. Return it to the large bowl and cover it with a clean cloth, then leave it somewhere warm and draught-free for about 45 minutes or until it has doubled in size.

4. Knock back the dough again for another couple of minutes and then divide it into 12 equal pieces. Roll each piece into a smooth ball and press a whole almond into the top. Place the rolls on a flat baking tray, about 2 in. apart. Cover them with a clean tea-towel and leave them in the warmth until they double in size again.

5. Bake at 400°F/200°C (Gas Mark 6) for 10 minutes, then reduce the heat to 350°F/180°C (Gas Mark 4) and continue to bake for a further 10 minutes.

APPLE CINNAMON ROLLS
(Makes 12)

Imperial (Metric)	American
2 oz (50g) fresh yeast	¼ cupful fresh yeast
1 dessertspoonful honey	1 tablespoonful honey
½ pint (¼ litre) warm water	1⅓ cupsful warm water
1 lb 6 oz (650g) wholemeal flour	5½ cupsful wholemeal flour
2 teaspoonsful ground cinnamon	2 teaspoonsful ground cinnamon
1 dessertspoonful sea salt	1 tablespoonful sea salt
1 medium-sized eating apple	1 medium-sized eating apple

1. Cream the fresh yeast and honey together with a fork and add the warm water. Blend the mixture well and set it in the warm to activate the yeast.

2. Put the flour, ground cinnamon and salt together in a large mixing bowl and combine them well. Grate the apple, including the skin, on a cheese grater and add it to the flour, mixing it in thoroughly.

3. Make a well in the centre of the flour and pour in the yeast mixture, stirring it in well to form a soft dough.

4. Turn the dough out onto a lightly floured board and knead it for 10 minutes. Return it to the bowl and set it in the warmth to let it prove.

5. When it has doubled in size, turn it back out onto the floured board and knead it for another few minutes. Divide the dough into 12 equal pieces and shape each piece of dough into a smooth ball by rolling it between the palms of your hands.

6. Place the rolls, evenly spaced apart, on a well oiled, flat baking tray. Leave the rolls in a warm place to rise again until twice their size.

7. Bake at 400°F/200°C (Gas Mark 6) for 15 minutes then reduce the heat to 350°F/180°C (Gas Mark 4) for another 10 minutes.

OATMEAL AND SESAME ROLLS
(Makes 12)

Imperial (Metric)	American
1 oz (25g) fresh yeast	2½ tablespoonsful fresh yeast
1 teaspoonful honey	1 teaspoonful honey
¼ pint (150ml) warm water	⅔ cupful warm water
¾ lb (350g) wholemeal flour	3 cupsful wholemeal flour
3 oz (75g) medium oatmeal	¾ cupful medium oatmeal
1 teaspoonful sea salt	1 teaspoonful sea salt
¼ pint (150ml) warm milk	⅔ cupful warm milk
A little extra milk	A little extra milk
½ oz (15g) sesame seeds	1 tablespoonful sesame seeds

1. Cream the yeast and honey together in a small bowl, add the warm water and mix it in well. Leave the mixture to bubble in the warmth for about 10 minutes.

2. Meanwhile, put the flour, oatmeal and salt into a large mixing bowl, make a well in the centre, and when the yeast liquid is ready, pour it into the well. Add the warm milk and mix it in to form a soft dough.

3. Turn the dough out onto a floured board and knead it for 10 minutes, using more flour if necessary. Put the dough back into the mixing bowl and cover it with a clean cloth, then put it in a warm place to rise for about 45 minutes.

4. When it has doubled in bulk, turn the dough out again and knead it for a further 2 or 3 minutes, then divide it into 12 equal pieces.

5. Shape each piece into a round, smooth ball by rolling it between the palms of your hands. Place the rolls on a flat, well oiled baking tray, about 1 to 2 in. apart, then let them rise for another 30 minutes in the warmth.

6. Brush the rolls with the extra milk and sprinkle the sesame seeds over the top. Bake them at 400°F/200°C (Gas Mark 6) for 10 minutes, then reduce the heat and bake them for a further 10 minutes at 350°F/180°C (Gas Mark 4).

WHOLEMEAL ROLLS WITH SPRING ONIONS AND CHIVES
(Makes 12)

Imperial (Metric)	American
1 oz (25g) dried yeast	2½ tablespoonsful dried yeast
1 dessertspoonful clear honey	1 tablespoonful clear honey
½ pint (¼ litre) warm water	1⅓ cupsful warm water
1 lb (½ kilo) wholemeal flour	4 cupsful wholemeal flour
1 teaspoonful sea salt	1 teaspoonful sea salt
2 oz (50g) fresh spring onions, finely chopped	⅔ cupful finely chopped fresh scallions
1 tablespoonful finely chopped fresh chives	1 tablespoonful finely chopped fresh chives

1. Put the dried yeast, honey and warm water together in a small bowl, blend them well and set the mixture aside in the warmth until the yeast starts bubbling.

2. Put the flour, salt, spring onions (scallions) and chives in a large mixing bowl and mix them together well. Add the frothy yeast mixture and stir it in thoroughly to form a dough.

3. Turn the dough out onto a well floured board and knead it for 10 minutes. Return the dough to the bowl, cover it with a cloth and leave it in a warm place until the dough has doubled in size.

4. Knock back the dough again for 2 or 3 more minutes until it returns to its former size, then divide it into 12 equal pieces. Knead each piece into a smooth, round ball and place them on a flat baking tray. Cover the rolls with a cloth and leave them to rise again.

5. When the rolls look puffy and well risen, bake them at 400°F/200°C (Gas Mark 6) for 10 to 15 minutes.

WHOLEMEAL ROLLS WITH RED BEANS
(Makes 12)

Imperial (Metric)	American
2 oz (50g) fresh yeast	¼ cupful fresh yeast
1 dessertspoonful clear honey	1 tablespoonful clear honey
½ pint (¼ litre) warm water	1⅓ cupsful warm water
1 lb (½ kilo) wholemeal flour	4 cupsful wholemeal flour
1 teaspoonful sesame salt	1 teaspoonful sesame salt
½ lb (¼ kilo) cooked red kidney beans, finely chopped	1⅓ cupsful cooked red kidney beans, finely chopped
A little beaten egg	A little beaten egg

1. Cream the fresh yeast and honey together in a small bowl, add the warm water and leave the mixture in a warm place to start frothing.

2. Put the flour, sesame salt and chopped red kidney beans into a large mixing bowl and stir them together well. Add the frothy yeast liquid to the flour and mix it in well to form a dough.

3. Turn the dough out onto a well floured board and knead it well for 10 to 15 minutes. Return the dough to the bowl, cover it with a cloth and leave it to rise in a warm place until doubled in size.

4. Knock back the dough again for another few minutes, then divide it into 12 equal pieces. Knead each piece into a smooth, round ball and place them on a baking tray. Cover the rolls with a cloth and leave them to rise again in a warm place until they look puffy.

5. Brush the tops of the rolls with the beaten egg and bake them at 400°F/200°C (Gas Mark 6) for 10 to 15 minutes.

SAVOURY PARTY FINGER ROLLS
(Makes 16)

Imperial (Metric)	American
1 oz (25g) fresh yeast	2½ tablespoonsful fresh yeast
1 teaspoonful honey	1 teaspoonful honey
¼ pint (150ml) warm water	⅔ cupful warm water
10 oz (300g) wholemeal flour	2½ cupsful wholemeal flour
1 teaspoonful sea salt	1 teaspoonful sea salt
2 dessertspoonsful skimmed milk powder	2 tablespoonsful skimmed milk powder
3 teaspoonsful yeast extract	3 teaspoonsful yeast extract

1. Mix the yeast, honey and warm water together in a small bowl and blend them thoroughly until the liquid is quite smooth. Leave the mixture in the warmth for about 10 minutes until the yeast begins to work.

2. Combine the flour, salt and skimmed milk powder in a large mixing bowl. When the yeast mixture is frothy, add the yeast extract to it and mix it well. Pour this mixture into the flour and blend them together until a dough is formed.

3. Knead the dough for about 10 minutes on a lightly floured board, then return it to the mixing bowl and cover it with a cloth. Set this aside in the warmth and leave it for approximately 45 minutes until it has doubled in size.

4. Knead the dough again for another couple of minutes, then divide it into 16 equal pieces. Roll each piece into a long, finger shape, about 5 in. long. Put them on a flat baking tray, spaced evenly apart, cover them with a cloth and leave them to rise again in a warm place.

5. When they look puffy and well risen, bake them at 400°F/200°C (Gas Mark 6) for about 10 minutes.

TIGER NUT FINGERS
(Makes 12)

Imperial (Metric)	American
2 oz (50g) fresh yeast	¼ cupful fresh yeast
1 dessertspoonful clear honey	1 tablespoonful clear honey
½ pint (¼ litre) warm water	1⅓ cupsful warm water
1 lb (½ kilo) wholemeal flour	4 cupsful wholemeal flour
1 dessertspoonful sesame salt	1 tablespoonful sesame salt
4 oz (100g) tiger nuts	¾ cupful tiger nuts
A little beaten egg	A little beaten egg

1. Cream the yeast and honey to a smooth paste. Add the water and stir it in well, then leave the mixture in a warm place to start bubbling.

2. Put the flour and sesame salt into a large mixing bowl and stir them together.

3. Grind the tiger nuts to a fine powder using a liquidizer or coffee grinder, and then mix it into the flour.

4. Add the frothy yeast mixture to the flour and mix it in to form a dough.

5. Turn the dough out onto a well floured board and knead it for 10 to 15 minutes. Return the dough to the bowl, cover it with a cloth and leave it to rise in a warm place until it has doubled in size.

6. Knock back the dough for another few minutes, then divide it into 12 equal pieces. Knead each piece into a 6 in. long 'finger' roll.

7. Place the rolls on a flat baking tray, spaced evenly apart, and brush them with the beaten egg, then leave them to rise in a warm place until the fingers look puffy and have nearly doubled in size again.

8. Bake the rolls at 400°F/200°C (Gas Mark 6) for 10 minutes.

ENRICHED EGG SHAMROCK ROLLS
(Makes 12)

Imperial (Metric)	American
1 oz (25g) dried yeast	2½ tablespoonsful dried yeast
½ pint (¼ litre) warm milk	1⅓ cupsful warm milk
1 dessertspoonful malt extract	1 tablespoonful malt extract
1½ lb (¾ kilo) wholemeal flour	6 cupsful wholemeal flour
1 dessertspoonful sea salt	1 tablespoonful sea salt
2 eggs, beaten	2 eggs, beaten
2 tablespoonsful sunflower oil	2½ tablespoonsful sunflower oil

1. Dissolve the yeast in the warm milk and add the malt extract, then leave the mixture in a warm place to start bubbling.

2. Put the flour and salt into a large bowl and mix them together well.

3. Add the beaten eggs and sunflower oil to the frothy yeast liquid and stir them in well. Pour the mixture into the flour and combine the ingredients to form a dough.

4. Knead the dough on a floured board for 10 to 15 minutes until it begins to feel more pliable, then return it to the bowl, cover it with a cloth and leave it in a warm place to rise.

5. Knock back the dough for a further few minutes, then divide it into 36 small, equal pieces. Knead each little piece of dough into a smooth, round ball and arrange them on a flat baking tray in groups of three, each group shaped like a shamrock. (Make a shallow slit on the top of each piece to represent the main vein in each leaf of the shamrock.)

6. Cover the rolls with a cloth and leave them to rise in a warm place. When the rolls look puffy, bake them at 400°F/200°C (Gas Mark 6) for 10 minutes. Reduce the heat to 350°F/180°C (Gas Mark 4) and continue to bake for a further 5 minutes.

STAFFORDSHIRE PEACH KNOTS
(Makes 12)

Imperial (Metric)	American
1 oz (25g) dried yeast	2½ tablespoonsful dried yeast
½ pint (¼ litre) warm water	1⅓ cupsful warm water
2 dessertspoonsful malt extract	2 tablespoonsful malt extract
1 lb (½ kilo) wholemeal flour	4 cupsful wholemeal flour
1 teaspoonful sea salt	1 teaspoonful sea salt
2 oz (50g) dried peaches, finely chopped	⅓ cupful finely chopped dried peaches

1. Dissolve the yeast in the warm water and add the malt extract. Stir the mixture well and leave it in a warm place for the yeast to start bubbling.

2. Put the flour, salt and chopped peaches into a large mixing bowl and combine them well.

3. Pour the frothy yeast mixture into the flour and stir it in well to form a dough.

4. Turn the dough out onto a floured board and knead it well for 10 to 15 minutes. Return the dough to the bowl, cover it with a cloth and leave it in a warm place to double in size.

4. Turn the dough out onto a floured board and knead it well for 10 to 15 minutes. Return the dough to the bowl, cover it with a cloth and leave it in a warm place to double in size.

5. Knock back the dough and divide it into 12 equal pieces. Roll each piece out into a long, thin strand, then tie each one into a Staffordshire Knot, as shown in the diagram.

6. Put the knots on a flat baking tray, cover them with a cloth and leave them to rise in a warm place. When the knots look puffy and well risen, bake them at 400°F/200°C (Gas Mark 6) for 10 minutes.

TOMATO AND ONION SPIRAL TWISTS
(Makes 12)

Tomato Dough

Imperial (Metric)	American
½ oz (15g) dried yeast	1 tablespoonful dried yeast
¼ pint (150ml) warm water	⅔ cupful warm water
1 dessertspoonful clear honey	1 tablespoonful clear honey
4 tablespoonsful tomato purée	⅓ cupful tomato paste
½ lb (¼ kilo) wholemeal flour	4 cupsful wholemeal flour
1 teaspoonful sea salt	1 teaspoonful sea salt

Onion Dough

Imperial (Metric)	American
½ oz (15g) dried yeast	1 tablespoonful dried yeast
¼ pint (150ml) warm water	⅔ cupful warm water
1 dessertspoonful malt extract	1 tablespoonful malt extract
½ oz (15g) dried onions	1 tablespoonful dried onions
1 clove garlic, crushed	1 clove garlic, crushed
½ lb (¼ kilo) wholemeal flour	4 cupsful wholemeal flour
1 teaspoonful onion salt	1 teaspoonful onion salt

1. Make the tomato dough as follows: dissolve the yeast in the warm water, add the honey and leave the mixture in a warm place for 10 minutes. Mix the tomato *purée* into the frothy yeast liquid and add this to the flour and salt, mixing well to form a dough.

2. Make the onion dough as follows: dissolve the yeast in the warm water, add the malt extract and leave the mixture in a warm place for 10 minutes. Soak the dried onions in boiling water for 5 to 10 minutes. Add the crushed garlic and reconstituted onion to the frothy yeast mixture and mix this into the flour and onion salt. Mix well to form a dough.

3. Knead both doughs well on a floured board for about 10 minutes, (if you're fairly ambidexterous you may be able to knead one with each hand at the same time, like they do in professional bakeries). Put the doughs into separate bowls, cover them with a cloth and leave them to double in bulk.

4. Knock back the doughs separately, then divide both sorts of dough into 12 equal pieces (24 altogether). Roll each piece into a 6 in. long strand. To make the spiral twists, take one strand of each colour, arrange them parallel to each other and fix the two ends together with a little cold water. Then twist the strands round and round until there are no gaps left between the two sorts of dough.

5. Put the twisty rolls onto a flat baking tray, spaced evenly apart. Cover them with a cloth and leave them to rise again in a warm place.

6. When the rolls look well risen and quite puffy, bake them at 400°F/200°C (Gas Mark 6) for 10 minutes. Reduce the heat to 350°F/180°C (Gas Mark 4) and continue to bake them for another 10 minutes until lightly browned on top.

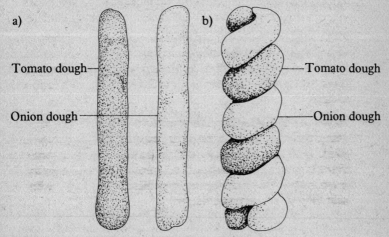

Fix together with a few drops of water at both ends.

OATFLAKE FARL
(Makes 2 small farls)

Imperial (Metric)	American
2 oz (50g) fresh yeast	¼ cupful fresh yeast
1 dessertspoonful honey	1 tablespoonful honey
½ pint (¼ litre) warm water	1⅓ cupsful warm water
1 lb (½ kilo) wholemeal flour	4 cupsful wholemeal flour
1 dessertspoonful sea salt	1 tablespoonful sea salt
3 oz (75g) porridge oatflakes	¾ cupful porridge oatflakes
A little vegetable oil	A little vegetable oil

1. Cream the fresh yeast and honey together in a small bowl. Add the warm water and mix it in well. Put the bowl somewhere warm and leave the mixture to start bubbling.

2. Put the flour, salt and 2½ oz (65g) of the porridge oats into a large mixing bowl and combine them well. Make a well in the centre of the flour and pour the yeast mixture into it, stirring it in thoroughly and working it into a ball.

3. Turn the dough out onto a floured surface and knead it for about 15 minutes until it starts to feel more elastic, then return it to the mixing bowl, cover it with a clean cloth and let it rise in the warmth for about 30-45 minutes.

4. Return the dough to the floured surface and knead it again for another few minutes, adding a little extra flour if it appears too sticky.

5. Divide the dough into two equal pieces and knead each one into a smooth ball, then place each one in a well oiled 8 in. cake tin and put them in the warmth for the second rising. When the dough seems to have doubled in size again, brush the surface of each farl with the vegetable oil and sprinkle the remaining oatflakes over the top.

6. Bake the farls at 400°F/200°C (Gas Mark 6) for 10 minutes, then reduce the heat to 350°F/180°C (Gas Mark 4) and continue to bake them for another 20 minutes until the crusts are golden brown.

NUTTY BAPS
(Makes 10)

Imperial (Metric)	American
2 oz (50g) fresh yeast	¼ cupful fresh yeast
1 dessertspoonful clear honey	1 tablespoonful clear honey
½ pint (¼ litre) warm water	1⅓ cupsful warm water
1 lb (½ kilo) wholemeal flour	4 cupsful wholemeal flour
1 dessertspoonful sea salt	1 tablespoonful sea salt
4 oz (100g) mixed nuts, chopped	¾ cupful chopped mixed nuts
A little beaten egg	A little beaten egg
2 extra dessertspoonsful mixed nuts, chopped	2 extra tablespoonsful chopped mixed nuts

1. Cream the yeast and honey in a small bowl using a fork and add the warm water. Stir the mixture well and leave it in a warm place until the yeast starts bubbling.

2. Put the flour, salt and the 4 oz (100g) of nuts into a large mixing bowl and combine them well. Add the frothy yeast mixture to the flour and mix it in well to form a dough.

3. Turn the dough out onto a well floured board and knead it for 10 to 15 minutes, using extra flour if it becomes too sticky. Return the dough to the bowl, cover it with a cloth and leave it in a warm place to double in bulk.

4. Knock back the dough again for another couple of minutes and then divide it into 10 equal pieces. Knead each piece into a round, smooth ball, then flatten it slightly to make into a bap shape.

5. Place the baps on a flat baking tray and leave them in a warm place to rise again. When they look well risen, brush the surface of each bap with the beaten egg and sprinkle the extra chopped nuts over the top.

6. Bake the baps at 400°F/200°C (Gas Mark 6) for 10 to 15 minutes.

DORSET BLUE CHEESE BAPS
(Makes 12)

Imperial (Metric)	American
1 oz (25g) dried yeast	2½ tablespoonsful dried yeast
½ pint (¼ litre) warm water	1⅓ cupsful warm water
1 dessertspoonful clear honey	1 tablespoonful clear honey
1 lb (½ kilo) wholemeal flour	4 cupsful wholemeal flour
1 dessertspoonful sea salt	1 tablespoonful sea salt
6 oz (150g) Dorset blue cheese	6 oz Dorset blue cheese
(or Stilton)	(or Stilton)

1. Dissolve the yeast in the warm water, add the honey and mix it in well. Set the mixture aside in a warm place to start frothing.

2. Put the flour and salt into a large mixing bowl and combine them well. Crumble the blue cheese into small pieces or grate it into the flour and mix it in thoroughly.

3. Add the yeast liquid and mix it in well to form a dough. Turn it out onto a floured board, cover it with a cloth and leave it in a warm place until doubled in size.

4. Knock back the dough for another few minutes until it returns to its former size. Divide the dough into 12 equal pieces and knead each piece into a smooth, round ball, then flatten it slightly to make it into a bap shape.

5. Place the baps evenly spaced apart on a flat baking tray, and leave them to rise again in a warm place.

6. When they look puffy and well risen, bake them at 400°F/200°C (Gas Mark 6) for 10 minutes, then reduce the heat to 350°F/180°C (Gas Mark 4) and continue to bake for a further 10 minutes until cooked through and lightly browned on top.

YEASTED FLATBREADS
(Makes 10)

Imperial (Metric)	American
½ oz (15g) fresh yeast	1 tablespoonful fresh yeast
1 dessertspoonful honey	1 tablespoonful honey
½ pint (¼ litre) warm water	1⅓ cupsful warm water
1 lb (½ kilo) wholemeal flour	4 cupsful wholemeal flour
1 teaspoonful sea salt	1 teaspoonful sea salt
2 tablespoonsful vegetable oil	2½ tablespoonsful vegetable oil

1. Cream the yeast into the honey and add the warm water, combining them well. Leave the mixture in a warm spot until the yeast starts bubbling.

2. Put the remaining dry ingredients into a large mixing bowl, add the vegetable oil and the yeasty liquid and mix them thoroughly to form a dough.

3. Knead the dough on a well floured surface for about 10 to 15 minutes until it feels more elastic. (Use plenty of extra flour if the dough seems to be too sticky.) Put the dough back into the bowl, cover it with a clean tea-towel and leave it somewhere warm and draught-free for about 45 minutes, or until it has doubled in bulk.

4. Knock back the dough for a couple of minutes, and then divide it into 10 equal pieces. Knead each piece individually for a minute or two to form a roll shape, then flatten each one between the palms of your hands until they are about ¼ in. thick.

5. Place the flatbreads on a well oiled, flat baking tray. (You may need two or three trays as the flatbreads are very large and round.) Leave them in the warmth, covered with a clean cloth, and when they start to look puffy and risen they are ready to bake.

6. Bake the flatbreads at 400°F/200°C (Gas Mark 6) for about 10 minutes and serve them warm with lots of butter.

SODA BREADS

WHOLEMEAL SODA BREAD
(Makes 1 round loaf)

All soda breads are quick and easy to make, so they are good recipes to use if you are in a hurry. However, they don't keep well for any length of time, so it's best to use them up on the day they are made.

Imperial (Metric)	American
1 lb (½ kilo) wholemeal flour	4 cupsful wholemeal flour
2 teaspoonsful sea salt	2 teaspoonsful sea salt
2 teaspoonsful bicarbonate of soda	2 teaspoonsful baking soda
½ pint (¼ litre) natural yogurt	1⅓ cupsful natural yogurt
¼ pint (150ml) warm water	⅔ cupful warm water

1. Place all the dry ingredients together in a large mixing bowl and combine them thoroughly. Add the yogurt and warm water and mix them in well with a fork.

2. Use your hands to press the ingredients together until a dough is formed.

3. Roll the dough lightly into a smooth ball and place it on a flat, well floured baking tray, then cut a deep cross over the top.

4. Cover the bread with a large bowl of some sort. (A *Pyrex* dish or a cake tin will do nicely as long as there is plenty of room for the bread to rise inside it.)

5. Put the bread straight into the oven and bake it at 400°F/200°C
    (Gas Mark 6) for 25 minutes. Then remove the cover from the
    bread and turn the oven down to 350°F/180°C (Gas Mark 4).
    Continue to bake the loaf for a further 20 minutes.

SPICED SODA LOAF
(Makes 1 round loaf)

Imperial (Metric)	American
14 oz (400g) wholemeal flour	3½ cupsful wholemeal flour
2 oz (50g) skimmed milk powder	⅔ cupful skimmed milk powder
2 teaspoonsful bicarbonate of soda	2 teaspoonsful baking soda
1 teaspoonful sea salt	1 teaspoonful sea salt
2 teaspoonsful ground cinnamon	2 teaspoonsful ground cinnamon
2 teaspoonsful ground nutmeg	2 teaspoonsful ground nutmeg
1 teaspoonful ground mixed spice	1 teaspoonful ground mixed spice
2 teaspoonsful lemon juice	2 teaspoonsful lemon juice
½ pint (¼ litre) milk	1⅓ cupsful milk

1. Put all the dry ingredients together in a large mixing bowl and
    combine them well.

2. Add the lemon juice and milk and mix them in to form a soft
    dough.

3. Knead the dough for a moment or two on a floured board and
    shape it into a smooth ball.

4. Place the loaf on a flat baking tray and cut a deep cross on the
    top.

5. Cover the dough with a large *Pyrex* dish or cake tin and bake it at
    450°F/230°C (Gas Mark 8) for 30 minutes.

RYE AND CINNAMON SODA LOAF
(Makes 1 round loaf)

Imperial (Metric)	American
10 oz (300g) wholemeal flour	2½ cupsful wholemeal flour
6 oz (150g) rye flour	1½ cupsful rye flour
1 dessertspoonful celery salt	1 tablespoonful celery salt
1 dessertspoonful ground cinnamon	1 tablespoonful ground cinnamon
2 teaspoonsful baking powder	2 teaspoonsful baking powder
½ pint (¼ litre) milk	1⅓ cupsful milk

1. Sift all the dry ingredients together into a large mixing bowl and combine them well.

2. Add the milk and mix it in to form a soft dough.

3. Knead the dough briefly, just enough to smooth out any creases and wrinkles in the dough.

4. Put the dough onto a flat baking tray and cut a deep cross in the top with a sharp knife.

5. Cover the loaf with a large *Pyrex* dish or cake tin and bake it at 450°F/230°C (Gas Mark 8) for 30 minutes.

LEXIA HONEY SODA BREAD
(Makes 1 round loaf)

Imperial (Metric)	American
1 lb 1 oz (525g) self-raising wholemeal flour	4¼ cupsful self-raising wholemeal flour
1 teaspoonful sea salt	1 teaspoonful sea salt
3 oz (75g) large Lexia raisins	½ cupful large Lexia raisins
1 dessertspoonful clear honey	1 tablespoonful clear honey
½ pint (¼ litre) milk	1⅓ cupsful milk

1. Put the flour, salt and raisins into a large mixing bowl, and combine them thoroughly, making sure that each raisin is individually coated with flour so that they won't stick together.

2. Stir the honey into the milk until it is dissolved. Add this liquid to the flour and mix it in to form a soft dough.

3. Knead the dough briefly on a floured board to smooth out any creases and shape it into a round ball.

4. Put the dough on a flat baking tray and make two deep slits in the form of a cross on the top.

5. Cover the loaf with a large *Pyrex* dish or cake tin and bake at 450°F/230°C (Gas Mark 8) for 30 minutes.

SODA FARL WITH RAISINS
(Makes 1 large round farl)

Imperial (Metric)	American
1 lb 4 oz (600g) wholemeal flour	5 cupsful wholemeal flour
2 teaspoonsful bicarbonate of soda	2 teaspoonsful baking soda
3 oz (75g) raisins	½ cupful raisins
2 teaspoonsful sea salt	2 teaspoonsful sea salt
¾ pint (400ml) milk	2 cupsful milk

1. Preheat the oven to 400°F/200°C (Gas Mark 6).

2. Put all the dry ingredients together in a bowl and mix them well. Add the milk and blend it in with a fork.

3. Use the hands to press the mixture against the sides of the bowl until a dough is formed.

4. Roll the dough into a smooth ball and place it on a well floured, flat baking tray. Cover it with a large cake tin or *Pyrex* dish, making sure that there is enough space inside for the bread to expand during baking.

5. Place the loaf straight into the oven and bake it at 400°F/200°C (Gas Mark 6) for 35 minutes. Remove the cover from the bread and reduce the heat to 350°F/180°C (Gas Mark 4). Continue to bake the loaf for a further 15 minutes and serve it warm spread with butter.

HERBED SODA BREAD
(Makes 1 round loaf)

Imperial (Metric)	American
1 lb (½ kilo) wholemeal flour	4 cupsful wholemeal flour
1 dessertspoonful sea salt	1 tablespoonsful sea salt
2 teaspoonsful bicarbonate of soda	2 teaspoonsful baking soda
1 dessertspoonful finely chopped fresh chives	1 tablespoonful finely chopped fresh chives
1 dessertspoonful finely chopped fresh parsley	1 tablespoonful finely chopped fresh parsley
1 dessertspoonful finely chopped fresh thyme	1 tablespoonful finely chopped fresh thyme
½ pint (¼ litre) milk	1⅓ cupsful milk
1 teaspoonful lemon juice	1 teaspoonful lemon juice

1. Put the flour, salt, bicarbonate of soda and chopped herbs into a large mixing bowl and combine them thoroughly.

2. Make a well in the centre of the flour mixture and pour in the milk and lemon juice, stirring it in with a fork until the dough starts to form.

3. Use your hands to round the dough into a smooth ball, using a little extra wholemeal flour if necessary.

4. Place the dough on a flat baking tray and make a shallow cross cut into the top of the loaf with a sharp knife.

5. Cover the loaf with a large *Pyrex* dish or cake tin and bake it at 450°F/230°C (Gas Mark 8) for 30 minutes, then remove the cover and continue to bake for a further 10 minutes.

FRUIT SODA FARL
(Makes 1 round farl)

Imperial (Metric)	American
1 lb (½ kilo) wholemeal flour	4 cupsful wholemeal flour
2 teaspoonsful baking powder	2 teaspoonsful baking soda
1 teaspoonful sea salt	1 teaspoonful sea salt
2 oz (50g) sultanas	⅓ cupful golden seedless raisins
1 oz (25g) currants	2½ tablespoonsful currants
½ pint (¼ litre) milk	1⅓ cupsful milk
1 teaspoonful cider vinegar	1 teaspoonful cider vinegar

1. Put the flour, baking powder, salt, sultanas and currants into a large mixing bowl and combine them well.

2. Make a well in the centre of the flour and pour the milk and vinegar into it.

3. Mix the ingredients well with a fork, then use your hands until the mixture turns into a soft dough.

4. Knead the dough briefly using a little extra wholemeal flour to make a smooth ball with no cracks on the outside.

5. Put the farl onto a flat baking tray and cut a deep cross in the top using a sharp knife. Cover the loaf with a large *Pyrex* dish or cake tin.

6. Bake the farl at 450°F/230°C (Gas Mark 8) for 30 minutes.

APPLE SODA FARL
(Makes 1 round farl)

Imperial (Metric)
1 lb (½ kilo) wholemeal flour
2 teaspoonsful bicarbonate of soda
1 teaspoonful sea salt
1 medium-sized eating apple
1 teaspoonful lemon juice
1 teaspoonful concentrated apple
   juice
½ pint (¼ litre) milk

American
4 cupsful wholemeal flour
2 teaspoonsful baking soda
1 teaspoonful sea salt
1 medium-sized eating apple
1 teaspoonful lemon juice
1 teaspoonful concentrated apple
   juice
1⅓ cupsful milk

1. Put the flour, soda and salt into a large mixing bowl and combine them well.

2. Grate the eating apple, including the skin and add it to the flour, mixing it in thoroughly.

3. Mix the lemon juice and concentrated apple juice into the milk, and then add the liquid to the flour.

4. Mix the ingredients well to form a dough and knead it very briefly so that it becomes smooth and round in shape.

5. Place the dough on a flat baking tray and cut a deep cross across the top of the loaf using a sharp knife.

6. Cover the loaf with a large *Pyrex* dish or cake tin and bake it at 450°F/230°C (Gas Mark 8) for 30 minutes.

INDIVIDUAL ALMOND SODA KNOBS
(Makes 8)

Imperial (Metric)	American
1 lb (½ kilo) wholemeal flour	4 cupsful wholemeal flour
1 teaspoonful sea salt	1 teaspoonful sea salt
2 teaspoonsful bicarbonate of soda	2 teaspoonsful baking soda
2 oz (50g) flaked almonds	½ cupful flaked almonds
2 teaspoonsful lemon juice	2 teaspoonsful lemon juice
½ pint (¼ litre) milk	1⅓ cupsful milk

1. Combine the flour, salt, soda and flaked almonds in a large mixing bowl.

2. Add the lemon juice and milk and mix them in to form a soft dough.

3. Knead the dough briefly and then divide it into 8 equal pieces. Roll each piece into a smooth ball and place them on a flat baking tray, spaced evenly apart.

4. Bake at 450°F/230°C (Gas Mark 8) for 15 minutes.

COTTAGE CHEESE SODA SCONE
(Makes 1 large, round scone)

Imperial (Metric)
6 oz (150g) cottage cheese with
  chives and onions
A little warm water
1 teaspoonful lemon juice
1 lb 2 oz (550g) wholemeal flour
1 dessertspoonful sea salt
2 teaspoonsful bicarbonate of soda
¼ pint (150ml) milk

American
¾ cupful cottage cheese with chives
  and onions
A little warm water
1 teaspoonful lemon juice
4½ cupsful wholemeal flour
1 tablespoonful sea salt
2 tablespoonsful baking soda
⅔ cupful milk

1. Put the cottage cheese into a measuring jug and add enough warm water to make it up to ½ pint (¼ litre). Add the lemon juice and stir it in well.

2. Put all the dry ingredients together into a large mixing bowl and combine them well. Add the cottage cheese mixture and the milk and stir them in thoroughly. Gradually draw the flour into the liquid until a dough is formed.

3. Shape the dough into a ball, and place it on a flat baking tray. Cover the loaf with a *Pyrex* dish or cake tin and bake it at 400°F/200°C (Gas Mark 6) for 15 minutes, then remove the cover from the bread and turn the heat down to 350°F/180°C (Gas Mark 4). Continue to bake the loaf for a further 35 to 40 minutes.

INDEX